MW00943628

Why Women Are Simply Better at Real Estate Investing

by Linda Baumgarten

Published in the United States by Ordinary To Extraordinary
Publishing, LLC
Milford, CT 06460
www.OrdinaryToExtraordinaryPublishing.com

ISBN-10:1536833606

This book is dedicated to my parents, especially Mom, who raised myself and my two sisters to be independent and self-sufficient women. You taught us that we can accomplish anything we set our sights on. You are a powerful role model for marriage and family. Be assured that your legacy lives on through us.

Acknowledgements

I HAVE SO MANY PEOPLE to thank for helping me create this book:

First and foremost, I am grateful to each of the real estate trainers I have worked with over the past thirteen years. You have shared your winning strategies and inspired me to invest in real estate. My special thanks go to Albert Lowry, Alan Cowgill, David Lindahl, Robyn Thompson, Tim Johnson, Elmer Diaz, and Robert Shemin. The coaching given to me by Speaking Empire was invaluable for crafting a powerful message from the stage and in front of the classroom.

Thank you to each contractor I have hired over the years. You showed up just when I needed you and did quality work. When you didn't do the job right, I learned how to make corrections and learned more about construction. From you, I learned how to manage teams, develop specific scopes of work, create budgets, buy materials, and work with building departments. Without you, I could not provide quality rental housing or buy/fix/sell real estate.

I appreciate the staff and volunteers at the Connecticut Real Estate Investors Association. Thank you also to CT REIA members and guests, and especially the Fast-Track Team Coaching students.

Your successes, as well as your in-the-field experiences, acted as a real life laboratory for investing in real estate. Not only did you accelerate my real estate learning curve and acquisitions, you also helped me develop the curriculum which trained so many of your classmates. You gave me the opportunity to do what I love to do best: coach, teach, and inspire individuals to be successful!

My deepest gratitude goes to Werner Erhard who gave me the gift of transformation, as well as all of the staff and seminar leaders at Landmark Worldwide with whom I worked to bring transformation to the world. Also thank you to T. Harv Eker who told me it was not only OK but my responsibility to be wealthy. I appreciate Brian Tracy for teaching me how to sell and to Zig Ziglar for teaching me to be proud of being a saleswoman. Also thank you to Marshall Sylver, Bob Proctor, and so many others.

I am so appreciative of my friend and best-selling writer Ginny Dye for encouraging me to write this book. Without you, I would never have considered becoming an author.

I honor the Girl Scouts of America. Growing up from Brownie to Juniors to Cadets to Seniors and then becoming a camp counselor, I discovered how to be a strong powerful woman who can accomplish anything I can imagine. I discovered management skills as a patrol leader, how to paddle a canoe in rapids and how to build a bonfire! What more could a girl want?

Last but not least, thank you to my life and business partner Barb Groel. You have been by my side as we have evolved through life. You are always my inspiration to be my best self. Reminding me that work is not everything, you remind me to exercise and eat my veggies! Thank you for being in my life.

Thank you for reading. I am excited to see the dreams you will fulfill!

Coming soon

Women are Simply Better at Getting Started Investing in Real Estate

Women are Simply Better at Marketing (November 2016)

Women are Simply Better at Finding Money to Buy Real Estate (January 2017)

Women are Simply Better at Rehabbing (April 2017)

Women are Simply Better at Creative Financing (July 2017)

Women are Simply Better at Selling and Negotiating (October 2017)

Women are Simply Better at Property Management (January 2018)

I invite you to visit us at www.WomenAreSimplyBetterAtIt.com to receive real estate and business resources, read excerpts and blog posts, and see news about these upcoming books.

Contents

Introduction

Are women really different?

I AM A BABY BOOMER, born in 1956. I came of age during the 60s, 70s, and 80s. This was an exciting time with lots of social upheaval here in America. Civil rights, gay rights, and women's rights.

My dad gave me nail polish and makeup when I was twelve. Most girls would have been thrilled but I wasn't. I wanted to be me without needing make-up or anything else. My dad also wanted me to learn typing and stenography so I could join the typing pool and always have a job. Now, I was really insulted. I was a 4.0 student and was NOT going to be a secretary.

I love my father. He raised my sisters and myself to be powerful women. At the same time, he was a product of the fifties. He thought he was taking care of me when he tried to make sure I had a fallback position.

My mother, on the other hand, wanted to raise us to be independent and self-sufficient women. She earned a Masters Degree in experimental psychology when it was rare for women to achieve such distinction. Although she was happily married to my father for forty-six years, she knew the world is an uncertain place. She wanted to ensure we could support ourselves if we needed to.

From an early age, I wanted to have the same opportunities as my men friends. I wanted to be man's equal in the working world I never once thought I couldn't get a job because I was a woman. I became a technical writer at one of the largest chemical companies in the world, and then an insurance saleswoman – when sales was really a man's world. Then I got started in real estate, not as a real estate agent but as an investor. This was unusual for a woman.

But recently, a transformation occurred. I started appreciating that being a woman actually is different than being a man in the business world. Not better, not worse, just different.

In 2003 I helped to found the Connecticut Real Estate Investors Association and the Connecticut Women's Real Estate Investors Association, and I started coaching real estate investors in 2009 As the students started having success, I invited them to share their success on stage. I began to notice that most of the success stories were told by women. For the first time, instead of trying to be equal to men, I began to discover the unique qualities that helped women be successful in real estate and in business.

By sharing what I've learned and observed, my hope is that you will identify your unique strengths and transfer them into being successful in real estate and as in business. This is the first of a series of books that will share these insights in a fun, simple straightforward approach. I have kept these books short. I have done this on purpose.

We are busy! We are already multi-tasking with family, job volunteering, and now starting a new career! My goal is to give you the heart of what you need so that you can get started fast making money with real estate. I intend to share with you the most effective strategies in the simplest terms with the most profitable results. And along the way, I will share stories about my own projects as well as about projects my friends and students have participated in.

You are extraordinary

Yes, ordinary women are extraordinary

TWENTY-FIVE YEARS AGO I declared to the world:

I am the possibility that ordinary people are extraordinary.

This declaration has shaped my life ever since. Since this life-changing moment, I have striven to identify the extraordinary qualities of each person I meet. Above all, I am committed to helping people recognize their extraordinary qualities. You will hear stories from some of these women in this book.

Simply being born makes you extraordinary. You are special and you are unique. Your opportunity, as you read this book, is to identify your unique qualities to give you power and to apply them to your new venture in real estate and in business.

Yes, you were born (almost always) with ten fingers and ten toes. You learned how to read and how to play. You made friends and you helped others along the way. Maybe you fell in love, established a home with your partner, and had children. Maybe you are single.

Along the way, you, an ordinary person, have done extraordinary things.

During the twentieth and twenty-first centuries, there have been so many firsts for women. They have now become congresswomen, senators, governors, prime ministers, Secretary of State (and other cabinet positions), CEOs, CFOs, COOs, physicians and pharmacists, and soldiers. Women have even become sports columnists, reporting from men's locker rooms. For the first time, women have earned the right to vote, to sign contracts and to apply for credit cards.

Women have become successful police officers, firefighters, and licensed tradespeople. In 1997 I attended the Women in the Trades and Non-traditional Occupations Conference. All around me were pioneering women who were learning how to do construction so they could join the unions.

As a woman you have always done what you needed to do to survive. You have taken the actions you needed to take to excel. As a woman you have had to do more than the guy next to you to gain respect, to get the grades, to get the pay raise and to get the promotion. You have taken extraordinary actions to take care of your family, your children, and your parents. As a woman, you have looked around your community and performed extraordinary acts of kindness to support your neighborhood, PTA, place of worship, and charitable organizations.

My mother is such an example of this. I am Jewish and my family celebrates Chanukah each year. Aside from presents, playing dreidel, and lighting the menorah, a favorite tradition is eating potato latkes (pancakes). Growing up, my sisters and I helped Mom grate the potatoes and onions, mix them with eggs and fry them on the griddle. When I was in first grade, Mom brought in enough latkes for my whole class. They were delicious! My teacher, Mrs. Gussie Seres was a short stout woman who was a force of nature. She asked Mom to come in and cook latkes for the Sunday school. Of course, Mom said yes, thinking she was making enough for our little class. Before she knew it, Mrs. Seres had somehow convinced Mom to make them for the entire Sunday school!

Does this sound familiar to you? How many cookies or cupcakes have you baked to raise money for your child's sports team or band? How many field trips have you chaperoned? How many car washes have you helped your teenager with? How many phone calls have you made to sign up other parents? How many marches, demonstrations or strikes have you attended? How many marathons have you walked, run or biked to raise money?

And how many causes have you supported, waiting for your opportunity? Historically, U.S. women supported the abolitionist movement in the 1800s, and then hoped the men would support them in their right to vote.

In the 60s (my coming of age), women demonstrated against the Vietnam war and fought for civil rights. And then hoped the men would support them in the Equal Rights Amendment. In the 80s and 90s, women organized and participated in AIDs marches to get medical care for and end discrimination against AIDs patients. And hoped men would support them in equal rights.

As women, we have been supportive of other folks. And now it's OUR turn. Our turn to pursue our dreams. Our turn to test our powers. Our turn to practice creativity. Our turn to create a business that will give us financial freedom and security.

The irony? As we become more and more successful, everyone else around us benefits. Our newfound success creates well-paying jobs, quality housing, role models and a legacy for generations to come.

This is what this series of books is about. How women can be, and are, successful entrepreneurs, especially in real estate. More importantly, I will give you the tools to be successful yourself. My dream is that you, an ordinary woman, will discover how extraordinary you really are.

Let's discover why women are better at real estate!

Women make the best entrepeneurs

The growth of women owned businesses is outstanding!

THE INTERNAL REVENUE SERVICE (IRS) makes an incredible amount of useful data available. I found a very interesting article called *U.S. Sole Proprietorships: A Gender Comparison, 1985-2000*. Although they have not updated it to more recent figures, the comparison is striking (bolding mine).

> While the **total number** of sole proprietorship businesses increased by 49.4 percent between 1985 and 2000, **the growth for female** sole proprietorships (81.5 percent) was more than twice that of male sole proprietorships (38.9 percent). Over the same time period, **business receipts** for female-owned sole proprietorships grew about three times more than those reported by sole proprietorships owned by men (76.4 percent compared with 25.2 percent). In comparison, **taxable profits** for male-owned sole proprietorships went up by 73.1 percent

over the same time period. (Growth rates are calculated using constant dollars.)[1]

The number of female sole proprietorships grew faster than that of their male counterparts at all levels of business receipts during 1985-2000. Unfortunately, although the growth and growth rates were very strong for women, men's profits were much higher than in women-owned businesses. This was especially true for businesses larger than $200,000.

> An average of 7.7 percent of male sole proprietorships made more than $200,000 in sales annually and accounted for 59.2 percent of their gross receipts each year. Female sole proprietorships were just 3.0 percent and 35.0 percent, respectively.
>
> Women have a strong showing with medium-sized firms (with receipts of $25,000 and under $200,000) accounted for 45.4 percent of total gross receipts for female sole proprietorships and 34.3 percent for male sole proprietors.[2]

During this period, a large percentage of women participated in door-to-door sales (19%) but only made 7% of what men made.

> In the most gender-segregated businesses, such as carpentering and floor contractor, female sole proprietorships grew 31.8 percent annually from 3,001 businesses to 13,626 businesses between 1985 and 2000, reaching a high of 24,401 businesses in 1994, while male child day care businesses grew 30 percent annually from 21,969 businesses in 1989 (the first year data were available) to 62,525 businesses in 2000.[3]

---

1 Lowrey, Ying, Tsinghua University, 2005, www.irs.gov/pub/irs-soi/00solprop.pdf (accessed July 19 2016).
2 Ibid.
3 Ibid.

Here is a very interesting statistic. Women were MOST competitive with men in REAL ESTATE ACTIVITIES. 13.5% of women and 12.37% of men were engaged in real estate.

Female real estate agents and brokers constituted the business activity where female sole proprietors were most competitive with their male counterparts in receiving the highest average net income. Women in this business activity had the highest average net income ($20,286) in all the major business activities; they were also comparatively close to profits reported by their male counterparts (representing 81.7 percent of men's average net income in the same business activity ($24,844)).[4]

Fast forward to 2012

According to the National Women's Business Council (which advises the United States President, Congress, and Small Business Administration), women-owned businesses increased by 26.8% between 2007 and 2012. This represents 36.3% of all non-farm and privately-held businesses (up from 26.8% in 2007). Although 89.5% of these businesses are sole proprietorships, women-owned businesses still created 8,431,614 jobs and generated $1.2 trillion in receipts![5]

---

4 Ibid.
5 "Women Owned Businesses Fact Sheet", National Women's Business Council, www.nwbc.gov/sites/default/files/FS_Women-Owned_Businesses.pdf (accessed July 6 2016).

Investing in women-owned businesses makes business sense

According to Goldman Sachs (bolding mine):

> Investing in women and girls is one of the highest return opportunities available in the developing world, as a wide range of economic research shows. Our own work has demonstrated that bringing more women into the labor force can significantly boost per capita income and GDP growth. **Our research has also shown that women's higher propensity to use their earnings and increased bargaining power to buy goods and services that improve family welfare can create a virtuous cycle:** female spending supports the development of human capital, which fuels economic growth in the years ahead.[6]

Currently, 70 percent of women owned businesses globally do not have access to financial products and services, such as savings accounts and loans. This leads to a global credit gap for women that IFC estimates to be close to $300 billion. Goldman Sachs' research paper called *Giving Credit Where It Is Due* shows that closing that gap could increase per capita income in emerging markets by an average of 12 percent by 2030. This gain could be as large as 25-28 percent for Brazil and Vietnam, where the credit gap in the formal SME[7] sectors are currently widest.[8]

---

6 Cai, Jin-Yong; Littlefield, Elizabeth L. and Powell, Diana Habib, "Unleashing the Power of Women Entrepeneurs around the World", *Huffington Post,* July 30 2015, www.huffingtonpost.com/jinyong-cai/closing-the-credit-gap-for women_b_7876314.html (accessed July 19 2016).
7 SME refers to small and medium enterprises.
8 Cai, Jin-Yong; Littlefield, Elizabeth L. and Powell, Diana Habib, *op cit.*

According to *The 2014 State of Women-Owned Businesses Report* commissioned by American Express OPEN:[9]

> As of 2014, it is estimated that there are nearly 9.1 million women-owned businesses in the United States, generating over $1.4 trillion in revenues and employing nearly 7.9 million people.
>
> Between 1997 and 2014, when the number of businesses in the United States increased by 47%, the number of women-owned firms increased by 68%—a rate 1½ times the national average. Indeed, the growth in the number (up 68%), employment (up 11%) and revenues (up 72%) of women-owned firms over the past 17 years exceeds the growth rates of all but the largest publicly traded firms, topping growth rates among all other privately held businesses over this period.
>
> Over the entire 17-year period from 1997 to 2014, there was an average of 591 new women-owned businesses started each day. In 2014, an estimated 1,288 new women-owned firms started each day during a single year.

Now it's YOUR turn!

---

9 "2014 State of Women-Owned Businesses Report", American Express OPEN, www.womenable.com/content/userfiles/2014_State_of_Women-owned_Businesses_public.pdf (accessed July 19 2016).

Creating a legacy

Taking care of your family & generations to come

WOMEN HAVE A STRONG NEED to take care of their family: children, parents, and siblings. Women, more than men, often feel compelled to put other people's needs ahead of their own.

In fact, aid agencies have found that the most effective use of funds is to give money to the women, especially to help them start a business or raise crops or raise animals. Women and mothers will make sure there is food on the table and their children are educated.

According to the Pew Research Center, in 2011 there were over three times the number of single mothers versus single fathers in the United States. (8.6 million women versus 2.6 million men in 2011).[10]

Why is this? Unfortunately, more men will abandon their kids while I suspect women feel compelled to stick around and make sure their children are taken care of, no matter what.

---

10 Livingston, Gretchen, "The Rise of Single Fathers", Pew Research Center, July 2 2013, www.pewsocialtrends.org/2013/07/02/the-rise-of-single-fathers/ (accessed July 19 2016).

Investing in real estate gives you the opportunity to create a legacy for your children, grandchildren, and great-great grandchildren.

Look at the legacy left by the Rockefellers. Generations of Rockefellers have lived a lifestyle many would be jealous of.

All this started with John D Rockefeller who founded the Standard Oil Company in 1870. Because of his success, he was able to build a legacy of targeted philanthropy including medical and educational institutions.

With real estate, you have the opportunity to create your own legacy. Buying rental properties will create cash flow and appreciation for generations to come. Do your children or grandchildren want to go to college or start a business? Why not buy a rental property in their name? The rents will pay for college, and then their own home and their retirement.

Want to start a philanthropy? You could buy a rental property and donate a portion of your profits from each flip to your favorite charity. Many of my friends have done this, contributing money to organizations that aim to save animals or end hunger.

You can use real estate to change your life and that of the generations which follow.

No such thing as family security or job security

There is an American traditional story that goes like this: A man and woman fall in love, get married, have 2.3 children, and buy a house in the suburbs with a white picket fence. The husband is the breadwinner, the wife a stay-at-home mom. The kids go to college. The spouses burn their mortgage when it is paid off after thirty years. The husband retires after thirty years with a full life-time pension. The happy couple eventually celebrates their fiftieth anniversary and gets their picture in the newspaper.

I am not sure how typical that was in the fifties when this story started. But it is rarely true anymore. Maybe you have experienced one of these life-changing events:

- → Becoming a single parent
- → Being part of a yours, mine, and ours family
- → Having children without being married
- → Being a stay-at-home dad
- → As a woman, being successful in a career and taking care of the house
- → Leading an alternative lifestyle
- → Becoming a widow
- → Your spouse being laid off, especially late in life
- → Having no pension
- → Depending on social security and your stock market acumen to live out your retirement years

If you have experienced one or more of these (or know someone who has) you know the myth of having a secure income with one job is just that – a myth.

My father worked for DuPont for thirty years. When he retired, he received a full pension and full medical benefits to support him and my mother. My story has been totally different. I read *Future Shock* by Alvin Toffler[11] before I graduated high school in 1974. In his book, Toffler predicted we would change jobs six or seven times during the course of our lifetime. This was a shocking concept at the time. However, this prediction would become my life story.

After graduating from college in 1979, I was hired and laid off four times in four years. In fact, a recruiter told me that if I didn't figure out a way to keep a job for a longer period, I would become unhireable! My longest position was five years.

Two weeks into my last job as a technical writer, I saw the writing on the wall. My supervisor, who had hired me, was met in her office by two security guards. She was told to pack up her personal items and was escorted from the building. Not only was she laid off, but she was faced with this indignity!

Every employee soon received a letter saying: "This company will be going through a transformation in the next ninety days. You may apply for up to three jobs including your current position. We will let you know if you are being moved to a new position, keeping your position, or being laid off."

I knew my days were numbered, once again

As I was looking for health insurance (contractors didn't receive benefits), the salesman invited me to come work for him. He represented benefits for entrepreneurs. For the first time in my life, I was totally dependent on commissions. For the first time in my life, I had my own business! Since I had to put food on the table, I had to teach myself how to sell. Let me tell you, I was a terrible salesperson! However, I found the best sales trainers in the world and listened to their tapes over and over again as I drove from appointment to appointment.

---

11 Toffler, Alvin, *Future Shock,* Random House, New York, 1970.

So I started my own business

I learned how to make appointments. This was in the "dark ages". No websites, no email. Just yellow pages, direct mail, and phone calls. By the way, back then we paid for every minute we were on the phone. Some months I faced a $900 phone bill! I paid $300 a month for Yellow Page advertising and coupon books.

I learned to have persistence and to know that every "no" put me closer to a "yes".

My job was to make a hundred phone calls a day, speak to ten to twenty people a day, set ten appointments a week, probably have two or three cancellations, and make three sales a week.

To keep track of my weekly progress, I used a white board or a piece of paper. I drew a hundred triangles, ten squares, and three flowers. I colored in a triangle every time I reached someone by phone or in person and a square each time I made an appointment. Happily, I colored in a flower each time I made a sale! (By the way, I also drew a stick each time I dialed the phone regardless of whether or not I reached the person. In this way, I acknowledged myself for taking action.)

I went from being broke to being the top representative in my region and being in the top ten in the country! I soon became a $3 million producer.

Once I learned how to sell and how to market, I knew I would never be laid off again. I might change products or might change situations, but I would never be broke.

Once I had my own business, there was no turning back. I knew I would be an entrepreneur forever. Being an entrepreneur means you can:

➤ Adjust quickly to the marketplace
➤ Start new businesses whenever you want
➤ Hire and fire people (including yourself, but more about that later)
➤ Create your own destiny

Failure is not an option

> A long while ago, a great warrior faced a situation which made it necessary for him to make a decision which insured his success on the battlefield. He was about to send his armies against a powerful foe, whose men outnumbered his own. He loaded his soldiers into boats, sailed to the enemy's country, unloaded soldiers and equipment, then gave the order to burn the ships that had carried them. Addressing his men before the first battle, he said, "You see the boats going up in smoke. That means that we cannot leave these shores alive unless we win! We now have no choice—we win, or we perish! They won. Every person who wins in any undertaking must be willing to burn his ships and cut all sources of retreat. Only by so doing can one be sure of maintaining that state of mind known as a BURNING DESIRE TO WIN, essential to success.
>
> Napoleon Hill, *Think and Grow Rich*

For most women, failure is not an option. When you have children, you must figure out a way to feed and clothe them. Whether you are single or married, you can no longer count on a company that will take care of you for the rest of your life. You HAVE to be successful just like the following three women who created their own success.

LS had always been the breadwinner. Her husband was a stay-at-home dad raising their three children. LS had a successful career in the financial world near New York City – until she was laid off. She had to find another career and fast. Not wanting to face a future of layoffs, she studied how to invest in real estate. Failure was not an option. She has become a successful rehabber on the Gold Coast of Connecticut.

MM and her husband had built a portfolio of rental properties while she worked for a large telecommunications company. She made a strong six-figure income but could see the writing on the wall. She needed to be prepared in case she was laid off. By the time she was offered a golden handshake to retire (a nice way of saying you are fired), she received training on how to raise capital and how to evaluate apartment buildings. She now runs a portfolio of 950 units in Georgia and her son, husband, and daughter are joining the business.

LA was a divorced mother of five and a grandmother of one. She had always liked renovating her own homes. When she realized it was time for her to make her own career, she turned to real estate. Since then, she has raised over $1 million in private funding, renovated houses, and purchased apartments. She said, "I made more money in this one deal than I had ever made in my entire life."

For these three women (and I know many more stories like these) real estate investing was the ticket to financial security and financial freedom. Even if your current life seems secure, I invite you to act as if you need a back-up plan.

I recently caught up with one of my students. She told me: "As you know, my husband and I started investing six years ago. Over the years we acquired 7 units, mostly through sweat equity. Although at the time he had a successful business and I had what seemed like a secure job at a local university, we always knew real estate investing was a smart thing to do.

Life circumstances can and did change in a heartbeat. His business dropped off a cliff, our marriage ended and my job is not so secure any more. Thank goodness for those cash flowing units!"

Having your own business is risky, isn't it?

In my opinion, you HAVE to have a back-up plan. Most people think being an entrepreneur is risky. But let me ask you, risky compared to what? We have already seen that having a job is not as secure as you want it to be. If your company loses a contract, outsources jobs to another country, or moves to another state, you are out of work and out of an income.

I am **not** suggesting you quit your job until you are ready and can afford to. I **am** saying that you want to start working on your job-exit strategy starting today. Aside from security, starting your own business gives you instantaneous tax benefits.

Ron Mueller, who shares tax-saving strategies to home-based business entrepreneurs, says that the United States tax code encourages entrepreneurship. He estimates that you can save $400 a month in taxes just by starting your own business! As a business owner, you can write off your home office, car mileage, office supplies, advertising, entertainment, travel and much more. Mueller goes on to say that the government wants you to have your own business as a backup to your 40 hour work week in case you get laid off![12]

At the time of the writing, the average tax savings on depreciating a three-family house is $4000 per year according to Ted Lanzaro, a CPA in Connecticut. He wrote:

> The typical accountant would take 20% of the house as land cost and the other 80% as building. Let's use an example of a rental property that is valued at $150,000. $150,000 x 80% is $120,000. The $120,000 building value is depreciated over 27.5 years for an annual depreciation of $4,364 per year.[13]

---

12   Mueller, Ron, *Home Business Tax Savings Learning Center*, www.homebusinesstaxsavings.com (accessed July 19 2016).
13 Personal correspondence.

This means you can make a profit from cash flow and still save money on your taxes! (Of course, please contact your CPA to discover exactly the amount for your situation.)

Real estate investing is risky, isn't it?

You can greatly reduce the risk in real estate by getting training to properly evaluate the transaction. You can also reduce the risk by having at least two exit strategies for each property.

For example, before you buy a single family house, ask yourself whether you can:

➤ Buy it, fix it and sell it quickly?

➤ Buy it, fix it, and sell it on a rent-to-own strategy?

➤ Buy it, fix it, and rent it for cash flow and long term wealth?

➤ Buy it, fix it, rent it, and then refinance your investment and still continue to collect positive cash flow?

If you see at least two exit strategies for each property, you will have a back-up plan. Our student WI shows a great example of this.

WI bought a house and rehabbed it. Just as he was putting it on the market, several other houses came up for sale on the same street. Rather than take a loss, he decided to lease it to a long-term tenant. When that tenant moved out several years later, the competition had died down. WI renovated the house and added a dormer. He was able to sell the house quickly for a sizable profit. In this case, rather than taking a loss, he was able to collect positive cash flow for several years, make a bigger profit, and saved money with long-term capital gains instead of short-term (less than one year) capital gains.

Take the shortcut: ask for directions

Men don't ask for directions, right?

You KNOW THE OLD JOKE. A man and a woman are driving to a party. The man thinks he knows how to get there. After the third time passing the same gas station, the woman insists on getting out and asking for directions. Turns out the house is two minutes away!

And how about setting up the bicycle Daddy bought for Jimmy or the doll house he bought for Janie on Christmas Day. Rather than reading the directions, Dad spends all day trying to figure it out on his own.

Before the days of the GPS and the smart phone, and just when the interstate highways were being built, my Dad would study the map and show me the route he had chosen to get us from Point A to Point B. Then, half an hour into the trip, he'd decide to follow a short cut he had just discovered. That "short cut" from Williamsburg, VA to my grandmother's house in Newport News lengthened our trip by an hour and a half!

Why don't men ask for directions?

To answer this age-old question, psychologist and success coach Linda Sapadin PhD wrote:[14]

> Men prefer to learn by doing, not by reading a book or being told what to do.
>
> Men want to win. They feel victorious when they figure out a solution on their own that makes sense to them.
>
> Men want to be strong. Asking for directions makes them feel vulnerable instead of in control of their world.

Asking for directions would be humiliating and mean admitting defeat.

But neither do women

I spent ten years of my life writing user manuals for engineering processes and software. What I discovered is that very few people ever open up the manual to seek out the answer. When was the last time you consulted the owner's manual in your car?

Have you noticed that manufacturers have stopped including manuals with their product. They give you a picture of how to set up the system and then tell you to go online if you need to download the manual. Maybe they figured out that no one reads the manual so why waste the paper and the money?

Gadget Helpline analyzed 75,000 calls received between September and October 2009 and discovered it's not just geeks who aren't reading the manual. A full 64 percent of men and 24 percent of women calling the line had not checked out the booklet that came with their computers or gadgets before picking up the phone.[15]

---

14 Sapadin, Linda, "Why Men Don's Ask for Directions", *Psych Central*, psychcentral.com/blog/archives/2014/03/23/why-men-dont-ask-for-directions (accessed July 16 2016).
15 Cheng, Jacqui, "Surprise! More Men Should Read the Freaking Manual", Ars Tenchnica, 9 November 2009, arstechnica.com/gadgets/2009/11/report-

What does this have to do with real estate?

What does asking for directions have to do with real estate? Everything. Every house, apartment building, or commercial building started with a blueprint that gives the design of each part of the building: foundation, structure, windows, roof, plumbing, electric, HVAC and more. The blueprint has to follow zoning regulations, fire codes and building codes. Without this plan, you don't have a building.

I gutted a four-family building. Totally. With a skillful team, I took down the walls and the stairs, ripped out the floors and even imploded the roof. All that was left was the basement and the shell of the house. It felt like a barn raising if you have ever been to one. Imagine standing in the basement and looking up at the sky!

At last, we started the process of rebuilding the building. The framers followed the blueprint exactly inch by inch to rebuild the structure. It was amazing to see this 2-D blueprint drawing come to life in 3-D.

Now what would happen if the framers did not follow the blueprint, did not follow the rules? Obviously there would not be a building. It would not pass the building inspection. More seriously, the building would not be safe if the framers had not followed the structural drawings. In fact, I had the architect and the structural engineer check it to make sure the real life structure lived up to the drawing.

Advantage: women

The advantage for most women is that we were not trained in construction or in the building trades. We *have* to ask for directions because we have no clue about the process. Even better, we are not expected to know. So when we ask a lot of questions of building inspectors or contractors, we usually get a good explanation.

---

men-need-to-read-the-manual-plug-stuff-in (accessed July 16 2016).

Warning: you can expect that they may talk to you like you are the little lady or the tough broad. Just ignore all innuendos Ask the questions you need to ask to have a successful project.

And if you don't understand the answer, keep asking the question in a different way until you fully understand what you need to understand.

After all, this is *your* project. Your name is on the deed or on the contract or on the lease. You are accountable for the success of the project. If you have a mentor, turn to her for advice BEFORE you sign the deed. Once you own it, you inherit the bad and the good.

A word to the men

If you are a man, you are expected to know construction Everyone thinks someone taught you how to fix things around the house and how to fix cars.

First of all, cars are so complicated today with computer gadgets that no one but a trained mechanic knows how to fix cars

Secondly, don't be intimidated. I have met (and hired) many licensed contractors who have made mistakes or who learned on the job. So be sure to ask questions and ask for directions so your project turns out on time, under budget and sells for a large profit.

How does this apply to non-construction?

Asking for directions applies to all parts of the real estate process There is a system to everything from mailing letters to posting signs to talking to sellers to negotiating deals. You get the idea.

When you ask for directions about how to send out mail, for example, you will discover:

➤ What kind of envelope to use (invitation)

➤ What kind of stationery (friendly, colorful, or yellow lined paper).

➤ What message to send (all kinds of discussion on this but I recommend you make it simple and personal)

➤ What kind of stamp (a real stamp)

➤ How should you address the envelope (write them out by hand or use a handwriting font)

➤ Who should you send them to? (lots of different kinds of lists, including people in your target area who no longer live in the house, for example)

When you follow these directions, your response rate will be anywhere from 5 to 20% instead of .05% – a big difference when you're investing $1 per mailer, right?

But sometimes asking for directions is expensive, isn't it?

If you are asking this question, you may be referring to manuals, seminars, and coaching/mastermind programs. Yes, these do come with tuition. However, over and over again, we have seen how the right instruction manuals and the right coaches can save you ten times over your investment.

Not asking for directions is also expensive

A while back, I bought a three-family house for only $30,000. It was a bargain but also needed a lot of work. I just started into the renovation without a plan and without much of a budget. I hired Joe the handyman who then hired other Joes and started to work. Finally, a licensed contractor came by and took pity on us. He finished the job and we were proud to rent this out for a very strong cash flow.

A year later, I took a course on rehabbing properties. Let's just say that if I had done the course first I would have saved at least $30k!

The course was $2,997. Saving $30,000 paid itself off ten-fold!

The nice thing about rental properties is that they are forgiving. You are collecting rent and over time your property will appreciate. However, if you are selling the property fast every dollar counts!

Of course, I would have not made any money if I had not also taken action! So congratulations on investing in this book and for taking action each and every day.

> Give me six hours to chop down a tree and I will spend the first four sharpening the axe.
> *Attributed to Abraham Lincoln*

Knowing the rules

L ET'S FACE IT: Little girls tend to be better at school than boys. I should know. I was the teacher's pet, the one who always raised her hand and knew the right answer. When I attended college, I was the one whose notes you wanted to copy so you could ace the exam.

When women grow up, we tend to be more interested in knowing the rules of the game. Women tend to buy more books, invest in more courses and invest in training.

As of January 2014, some 76% of American adults ages 18 and older said that they read at least one book in the past year. Women were more likely than men to have read a book in the previous 12 months (82% versus 69%). [16]

More importantly, women tend to follow the instructions they learned in that education and tend to ask more questions to make sure they understand what they need to understand.

---

16 Zickhur, Kathryn and Rainie, Lee, "A Snapshot of Reading in America 2015", Pew Research Center, January 6 2014, www.pewinternet.org/2014/01/16/a-snapshot-of-reading-in-america-in-2013/ (accessed July 16 2016).

Monopoly

When I was a kid, I used to play Monopoly for hours on end (Maybe playing this game created my first love of real estate!) I learned how to win by learning the rules of the game.

→ Land on a property and buy it

→ Buy four houses and get a hotel

→ Get money every time another player lands on my property

After learning the rules, I then developed strategies for winning the game.

→ Should I buy the blue properties which were the most expensive and yet gave me the highest rent?

→ Or should I buy multiple properties at lower price points so I could dominate the block?

→ Should I buy every property I land on or select the properties I wanted?

→ What about the utilities and the railroads?

Of course, as in life, there was the element of chance.

→ Could I roll a double three and land on Free Parking?

→ What if I drew the wrong card in Community Chest and ended up paying hospital fees of $100?

→ Or drew the Chance card which landed me on Illinois Avenue which could be good or bad?

Then my sisters and I invented our own Monopoly credit cards so that we could borrow money to pay utilities and mortgages when we ran out of play money. (Bills under $200 had to be paid off when your piece passed Go.) We improvised so we could make more deals.

All of this started by knowing the rules of the game.

Rinse and repeat

Women have been following instructions since they first started washing their hair. I read on the back of a Pantene shampoo bottle:

> Dispense into palm and rub hands together. Apply shampoo to wet hair, massaging scalp with fingertips in a rotating motion. Work lather through to ends. **Rinse thoroughly and repeat if desired.**

In other words, follow the instructions, get the results and do it again.

How many times have you wondered why airline stewards tell you how to put on your seatbelt? Don't we all know how to do this?

Well what happens if you're in an accident? Won't you be happy that you put on your seatbelt in the right way?

So what does this have to do with real estate? And why do women have the advantage?

Real estate is a rinse and repeat business

While there are many styles of houses and apartment buildings, 90% of this business is the same. When you learn how to rinse and repeat you will:

- ➔ Save time because you have systems and procedures in place
- ➔ Save money because you can buy material in bulk and hire the same contractors to do the same work
- ➔ Make more profits as you know what sells in your market
- ➔ You can buy/sell or buy/rent more than your competition

Warning: As entrepreneurs, we love to create. We love to reinvent the wheel. However, this is not how you make money. Find out the rules and stick to them. It may be boring, but you won't be bored as you're driving to the bank to cash those checks!

I love this quote from Charlie Parker. It reminds me of when I played piano as a young person. I practiced scales every day. I studied music theory so I understood how the music was created. I practiced each part of the music piece until I memorized it. Then when I was in concert, I could relax and really feel the music as I performed to the audience.

This quote also reminds me to do the basics so that I am prepared for any real estate situation. Practice your scripts. Do your due diligence. Do a thorough scope of work. Study real estate trends for your location. Then when you are in a non routine situation and have to think fast, you can rely on your training to create the correct response.

> You've got to learn your instrument. Then, you practice, practice, practice. And then, when you finally get up there on the bandstand, forget all that and just wail.
>
> *Charlie Parker, Jazz musician*

Model your business after successful people

Learn from the School of Hard Knocks OR model yourself after someone successful

Unless you were born in the trades and your family was in construction, you have to learn this business from someone. You will either learn on your own in the School of Hard Knocks or you will be lucky enough to find a mentor to teach you the ropes. Earlier I shared with you how an experienced contractor rescued me when he helped me finish renovating a three-family house. I also shared that if I had received instruction first, I estimate that I would have saved $30,000.

To avoid the School of Hard Knocks, work for a construction company as a gofer, tradesperson or job estimator. For apartments, work for a property management company. How about doing grunt work with an investor-friendly real estate agent? Consider volunteering with Habitat for Humanity where you can get hands-on experience building houses.

Interview the investors in your town. One of the biggest apartment owners in my town exercised in the same gym as myself. Fortunately, he was well-respected in town so I learned the right way to offer quality housing in the inner city. Be aware, however, that most successful rehabbers and apartment owners are very busy and do not have much time for inexperienced people. Many times, they are afraid of the competition and keep their inside secrets to themselves. Be aware that some of them do business the right way and some of them do not.

To find people you can model and who are accountable for your progress, attend your local real estate investor association. Check out their reputation for training and instruction. For example, the Connecticut Real Estate Investors Association offers the Fast-Track Team Coaching Program and has created many successful entrepreneurs. Local mentors are usually the best because they know your market and can connect you with lenders and contractors. However, you may want to search out-of-area for someone with a certain specialty or reputation especially if you cannot find local coaches.

Systems: saving yourself time, energy and money

When you build a house, you build the foundation first, then you frame it, then you put on the roof. It would look ridiculous if you put the roof on first. The same is true when you are talking to a seller. Most people meet a seller over the phone and make an offer without seeing the house and without creating a relationship with him or her. That is totally backwards.

When you understand the rules, and when you understand the reasoning behind the rules, you can duplicate the success of other people and you will reach success faster. For example there is a system to rehabbing houses:

1. Walk the entire property
2. Take detailed photographs and measurements
3. Make a list of everything that needs to be repaired, torn down or replaced.
4. Check out the competition
   a. For example, we replaced every single window with vinyl windows. I found out later that if the other houses in the neighborhood don't have new windows, you don't have to put them in either.
   b. One friend of mine tore out oak cabinets and installed brand new cherry cabinets with granite countertops. They looked beautiful. However, the neighborhood did not require such a nice kitchen and she wasted $10,000 that should have gone into her pocket.
5. Negotiate with the contractors
6. Set up the timeline
7. Set up your budget

8. Manage the project to completion
9. Cash your check that you receive at the closing when you sell the property
10. Rinse and repeat

Following the rules and following a system means you can save yourself time and increase your profits. You can repeat your success over and over again. You can start hiring other people to take over parts of the business. (HINT: Only give away parts of the business to each person. You want to be the mastermind of your operation and not training your competition.)

Now you are a business owner which means you can make money even when you are not actively working. The faster you can duplicate and triplicate your actions, the faster you can make more money. In other words, if you have a system in place for rehabbing houses, you can be working on two, three or more projects at the same time.

I don't know who created this acronym for SYSTEM but it certainly works doesn't it?

Save Your Self Time Energy and Money

Checklists, blueprints, procedures and more

As you continue reading the books in this series, you will be learning systems for making money in real estate. I will be sharing checklists, scripts, procedures and more that you can adapt to your own personality and to your own business.

For example, in *Women are Simply Better at Getting Started in Real Estate,* I will be giving you a checklist for estimating the repairs on a house. The checklist will help you remember everything to look at while walking through the property. Without using a checklist like this, you will be winging it. In my experience, winging it can cost you $5,000, $10,000 or more because you missed something or you totally forgot to check something in the house.

35

One of my friends was so excited to buy a house from an experienced renovator. It was going to be her very first project. She trusted them to come up with the list of repairs. Unfortunately, she did not get a home inspector or other contractor to go over the property with a fine tooth comb. During a heavy rainstorm, she discovered water coming through the roof! She found out that the chimney bricks were in bad shape. She had to rebuild the chimney and replace much plywood on the roof before putting down new roof shingles. If she had only done her due diligence, she would have negotiated a lower price on the property. She also would have finished the project much faster because she would not have had this big surprise.

Here is another acronym: SWAG which means "scientific wild-a** guess". (By the way, apparently SWAG also means Southern Women Aging Gracefully.) When you don't use a checklist, your estimate of repairs is a SWAG.

Hiring a contractor does not replace your system. I have seen so many contractors give me a SWAG estimate only to tell me later that they forgot to incorporate this or that repair, or that they didn't measure the size of the kitchen, or that the materials were more expensive than they thought.

To avoid a SWAG estimate of repairs:

➤ Be systematic as you walk through the property.

➤ Take lots of photos so that you can refer to them when you get home. My students often send me 50-100 pictures.

➤ Ask a contractor to walk through the property thoroughly. Often these contractors will do this for free hoping that you will hire them to do the work.

➤ When you find a property you are serious about buying, you could hire a licensed home inspector and/or structural engineer. Be sure that the home inspector has many years of construction experience.

➤ You also want to test buried oil tanks, septic systems, and wells. These items can be very expensive to repair.

➤ You may also want to hire a surveyor to confirm the boundaries of the property.

➤ Finally, you are going to check for any open building permits and any fire or health violations that you need to take care.

You will be discovering systems for marketing, for determining the value of a property, for real estate legal documents, for tax write-offs, and so much more.

Remember this:

SWAG = losing money

Knowing the Rules and Following Them = Making Money

Be sure to take the time to learn the rules and be sure to have checklists or blueprints or systems to make sure you follow the rules.

Multi-tasking, juggling & focusing

Women tend to be better at multi-tasking

> Definition of multi-tasking:
> The concurrent performance of several jobs by a computer
> The performance of multiple tasks at one time
>
> *Merriam-Webster Dictionary*

DOES YOUR TYPICAL MORNING look like this? Wake up with the alarm, put on the coffee pot, wake up your kids and your spouse, make breakfast, make lunch, get everyone dressed, sign Natasha's permission slip for the field trip, remind Carlos to grab his homework, remind your spouse to pick up the kids after school, and get everyone out the door on time?

Whew! And it's only 8 am!

Now you go to the office, turn on the computer, look at your calendar and start checking off things on your to-do list. Fifteen minutes later, your boss comes in and gives you a new task that just must get done today, your secretary tells you an important phone call is coming in and the caller just won't take no for an answer, and your emails are crying for attention.

And that's just the start of your day!

Sound familiar?

As women, we tend to be able to handle many tasks at once. We plan for events more and we are better able to switch quicker between tasks.

Maybe we need to be able to do this to survive. Remember the statistic that there are four times as many single mothers as single fathers? That means we need to handle all of the family tasks as well as the job tasks for survival.

Is multi-tasking a real thing?

When you look at the definition, multi-tasking refers to a computer doing multiple tasks at the same time. Can we mortal human beings do the same thing?

Although I pride myself on being able to multi-task, I must admit that I don't multi-task at any one point in time. I do handle a lot of tasks in many different projects in one day.

Have you ever watched martial arts movies? Look at Jackie Chan, or the Karate Kid for example. They are surrounded by thugs. One against many. At first, it looks like they are fighting off everyone at once. When you look at the film again slowly you see that they fight one person at a time very quickly. They fight off one person, being aware of the others, and rapidly respond to each attack in quick succession.

That is what we do as women. Look at the office example I described earlier. How do you handle this situation at your job?

- ➤ Prioritize – quickly prioritize each situation.
- ➤ Plan – If you're honest with yourself, you realize you shouldn't be surprised because your boss often comes at you with emergency requests and you can allow time for them

Another advantage to planning is that the routine and mundane items are already in the works so that you can react quickly when last minute items arrive.

➤ Make decisions quickly.
➤ Take action immediately.
➤ Focus on one thing at a time and be prepared to move back to the situation at hand.

It is the switching back and forth between tasks where women seem to be better than men.

Dr. Gijsbert Stoet of the University of Glasgow and Prof Keith Laws of the University of Hertfordshire studied multi-tasking tasks between men and women in several tests.

Dr. Gijsbert Stoet said: "Multitasking is [becoming] more and more important in the office."

In a test where Dr. Stoet had men and women switch back and forth between counting tasks and shape-recognition tasks, women were 8% faster than men. (Men and women were equal when they were able to do one task at a time. "It could be that men suffer more from this constant switching," Dr. Stoet said.

In another test, a group of women and men were given eight minutes to complete a series of tasks – locating restaurants on a map, doing simple math problems, answering a phone call, and deciding how they would search for a lost key in a field.

Completing all these assignments in eight minutes was impossible – so it forced men and women to prioritise, organise their time, and keep calm under pressure.

"Women spent more time thinking at the beginning, whereas men had a slight impulsiveness, they jumped in too quickly," said Prof Laws.

"It suggests that - in a stressed and complex situation – women are more able to stop and think about what's going on in front of them." Maybe this strength is derived from the earliest of times when women had to balance home, cooking, and tending to children whereas men could focus solely on hunting.[17]

How does this work in real estate?

Remember when I told you that your life experiences will help you be successful in real estate? Well, your experience in managing your family or your job will certainly come in handy

When I rehabbed my first house, I was surprised at the many many decisions I had to make. Although I made a detailed list of everything that needed to be done (also known as a scope of work), I still had to make decisions on-the-fly.

Teamwork

When you are renovating a property, you have multiple contractors working on site. Sometimes you will have carpenters plumbers, and electricians there at the same time. It is almost like you are conducting an orchestra. If any one person doesn't do their job, it can delay everyone else's productivity.

As the CEO of your rehab, you need to make sure each contractor does her job and communicates with you when there is an issue.

I have found that all contractors (mostly men, by the way) love to complain about each other. They love to show me how someone else did not do something the right way.

For example, my general contractor loved to complain about the painter and the electrician because they were not the ones he normally used as part of his team. Then he would demonstrate how he was the hero because he made sure they corrected the issue.

---

17 Morgan, James, BBC News, October 24 2013, www.bbc.com/news/ science-environment-24645100

This kind of tattletaling can be annoying. However, it can be useful also as you find out about concerns that you would not have known about otherwise.

If you are a parent, this will seem familiar to you. How many fights among your children have you needed to referee? How many times have you told them to work it out amongst themselves? And when have you had to get involved directly?

You can deal with tenants, contractors and other staff in the same way.

Your job as CEO is to ensure that:

➤ There is open communication between the contractors and you

➤ The contractors are clear about their task, including the materials they are to use

➤ The contractors are clear about the timeline and deadlines and the importance of keeping them

➤ Any change orders are in writing

Multi-tasking in your real estate business

Aside from managing multiple tasks while rehabbing a property, you need to multi-task in your business.

First of all, you are already dealing with your family and job responsibilities. So you will be quickly sorting back and forth between business and family. It is very important for you to schedule time for the important things in your life. Set up dates with your kids and your special person. Schedule time for exercise, religious and spiritual activities, and fun!

I recommend you call a family meeting and let them know that you will be busier than ever. Then tell them why you are creating this business. Each member of your family needs to see what's in it for them. You might want to create a special vacation when you complete your first real estate project. If you have teenagers, a rental property could give them the freedom to attend the college of their choice. Perhaps your spouse can retire early through this business. You get the idea.

Then in your business itself, you will be multi-tasking Unfortunately, this is how life usually goes:

> You focus on marketing, marketing, marketing like I show you in *Why Women Are Simply Better at Getting Started in Real Estate.*
>
> Hurray! You put a house under contract. Now you focus on the due diligence and gathering rehab estimates.
>
> Oops! You need more money so you focus on finding private money, hard money, credit cards and whatever it takes.
>
> As soon as you buy the house, you are totally focused on managing contractors and building inspectors.
>
> Hurray! You have a beautiful property. Now you are laser focused on selling or renting it so you can pay off the loans and cash in your profit.
>
> Whew! You celebrate!
>
> Tomorrow you wake up and realize you don't have another project in your pipeline. So you focus on marketing, marketing, marketing. And the cycle begins again.

To run a business, you have to have your focus on everything I just described *all the time.* When you are able to juggle multiple facets of the business, you will always have properties in your pipeline. You will be making money throughout the year.

This is why multi-tasking is so important. As we discussed earlier, you cannot do more than one task at any one moment However, you can set up a system which allows you to see the status and progress of each part of the business. You will prioritize, delegate, and manage people and tasks.

Of course, this comes with experience. If you are a project manager in your job, you can transfer those skills into your business. If not, take it one step at a time and you will achieve this goal.

Negotiate your way to big profits

> Negotiate:
> To discuss something formally in order to make an agreement
> To agree on (something) by formally discussing it
> To get over, through, or around (something) successfully
>
> *Merriam-Webster Dictionary*

Why negotiate?

Deals are not given to you. You need to create them.

Negotiation is the way to do that. Of course, you can negotiate the price.

Did you also know you can negotiate the terms of the transaction? For example, you can negotiate terms on any of these facets of the deal:

Owner financing	Cash flow
Tax benefits	Timeline
Interest rate	Down payment

Anyone can offer a lowball offer and eventually get one (out of a hundred offers) accepted. In fact, there are many people in the industry who say, "If you aren't embarrassed about your offer you're offering too much."

One of my students told me she had wasted a year, sending hundreds and hundreds of blind lowball offers and none of them were accepted. She wasted a year without buying one piece of real estate. Along the way, she burned a lot of bridges with real estate agents and sellers.

Sometimes this strategy works. For example, one of my students wholesaled several properties a month. He would send out offers at 50% of the Multiple Listing Service (MLS) listing price through an automated system. (The MLS is the database of properties for sale that are listed by real estate agents.) These properties had been on the market for six months or more and the sellers were getting motivated. (Wholesaling is the art of putting a property under contract and then assigning that contract to someone else at a higher price.)

Most of the time, his real estate agent received hate mail Every once in a while, his realtor would find a buyer who was interested in the offer. And then the negotiations would begin (By the way, I don't understand why real estate agents get upset If my client's property had been listed for more than six months I would be anxious to see all offers and negotiate from there.)

When the agent decided to close his own brokerage for personal reasons and join one of the franchise brokerages, his new boss said he couldn't make these blind offers because of all the negative feedback.

Again, I am not saying you shouldn't make lowball offers, I am saying there may be many more effective ways to get what you want.

Can women be successful salespeople?

When I first started my career in insurance sales, almost all of the other salespeople were men. Over time, however, more and more women joined our ranks. Even more importantly, more women started winning top sales awards.

Sales has traditionally been a man's world. Women are only making 62% of what male salespeople make. So we certainly have some challenges. The difference in compensation is not necessarily a result of blatant discrimination. In any sales organization, men and women earn the same percentage for commission. (In other words, male and female real estate agents both earn 6% when they sell a house.) So why is there so much of a difference in actual compensation? Much of the difference in compensation has to do with the types of clients men have versus the clients that women typically have:

> In a study of two large stock brokerages, Wharton professor Janice Madden found that saleswomen earned less than salesmen because they'd been systematically given inferior accounts that generated smaller commissions.[18]

So it can be said that, on level terms, women are just as successful if not more successful than men. Fortunately, real estate allows you to select your market and your own staff. If women are earning less than men, it could be that their listings are at a lower price point than men.

As women, we have some strengths going for us. However, we also have some challenges.

---

18 "Women in the Workplace: A Research Roundup", Harvard Business Review, September 2013, hbr.org/2013/09/women-in-the-workplace-a-research-roundup (accessed July 16 2016).

Negotiating challenges for women

Women tend to have less confidence when it comes to sales and negotiation. Maybe it is the way we are raised or a result of our life experiences. Either way, men tend to be more outgoing, less afraid of rejection and more willing to take risks.

Fear of rejection

Let's look at baseball. The most highly paid baseball players carry a batting average of around .300 or 30%. What does this mean? Seventy percent of the time, the batter fails to hit a ball and get on base!

Most of the time, we give up after making a few phone calls We don't like being rejected. We are afraid the person on the other end of the line is going to be mad at us or hang up on us (By the way, I am ALWAYS nice to telemarketers – they have a very tough job!) If you follow the baseball analogy, you need to talk to a hundred people to have thirty yeses. And, in today's world of caller ID, you may have to dial a thousand people to talk to a hundred people to get thirty yeses.

Lack of confidence

As mentioned above, men tend to get assigned to the bigger accounts. In the corporate world, this means men are more likely to be assigned to C-level executives who make the big decisions: CEOs, CFOs and COOs.

As an entrepreneur, you can go after any clients as you want That means you can buy a $15,000 property or a $1.5 million apartment complex. You can also buy a property at 90% of fair market value or 30% of fair market value. Similarly, you can negotiate with a contractor to do the job for $18,000 or $9,000

Much of this has to do with your confidence in approaching the decision makers and in asking for what you want.

How do you become more confident?

I will never forget our student ST. She and her husband wanted to buy multi-family houses for positive cash flow. One way to find off-market rental properties really quickly is to call rental ads. When you call the ad, you ask if the owner is interested in selling the property instead of just renting it. If so, then you move forward along the path of buying the property. Well, ST heard this strategy. She was terrified to pick up the phone. She was afraid of being rejected; she was afraid the landlord would get annoyed and hang up. In fact, she called the phone the "two ton gorilla"! Here is where it gets good. ST picked up the phone anyway. Each time she made a phone call, the phone got lighter. She and her husband soon purchased a three-family with a Christmas tree farm. Since then, they have purchased at least two other rental properties.

She was so happy she picked up the two ton gorilla. Will you pick up the phone?

When you are brand new in real estate, you may not be feeling sure of yourself. You have to figure out a way to work through that so that you can make offers and buy properties.

Once you start having success, each phone call or offer or renovation becomes easier.

One strategy is to *fake it till you make it*. If you act like you know what you are talking about, the other person will believe you.

Let's do an exercise: Think of a successful real estate investor or entrepreneur you know, someone you admire.

How do they carry themselves?
What do they wear?
How do they talk?
What phrases do they use?

Become that person. Mimic his/her conversations, mannerisms, and confidence. Over time, you will blend in your own personality and create your own secret to success. If this person is a trainer, I encourage you to listen to their tapes/CDs/MP3s in your car over and over again. You will hear their words coming out of your mouth.

You know more than the other person

Another way to increase confidence is to remember that you are simply buying a house or property from another person. As you will see later, the more you portray yourself as a regular, everyday person, the better the terms you will be able to negotiate.

Be yourself. Remember that you usually know more about real estate than your seller. They are looking for you to provide the solution to their problems.

Toot your own horn

I still remember my mother saying, "Honey, it's not polite to brag". Sound familiar? Unfortunately, that advice usually works the other way. We go overboard in the other direction. Instead of acknowledging ourselves, we promote our limitations and doubts.

Well, I am here to give you permission to brag. It is time for you to acknowledge yourself for your successes, no matter how small.

Each day make a list of five successes. They could be as small as "I sent marketing letters today" or as big as "I just put my first house under contract." By acknowledging your progress each day, you will feel more and more successful. You will see rapid success.

Create a credibility package

Create a credibility package. Your credibility package is designed to provide your credibility to people with whom you want to do business. You will present this to private lenders, banks, and sellers. We will discuss this in more detail in *Women are Simply Better at Finding Money to Buy Real Estate.*

If you are brand new at real estate, treat your credibility package as your professional resume. List each employer along with the tasks you performed. Highlight the tasks that have any kind of commonality with real estate.

If you have ever purchased real estate (even your own home), show before and after photos. Show what you purchased it for, cost of repairs, how much you sold it for, or how much cash flow and appreciation you have for the rental property.[19]

If you have good credit (a 720 or more score), you might want to include your credit report. You can also include your assets such as retirement accounts. You can also include community activities, volunteer work, awards, and commendations, as well as personal testimonials.

By the time you have completed this document, you will be even more impressed with yourself. Whether you use this or not in a negotiation, you will have ten times more confidence in yourself.

---

19 Appreciation refers to the increase in value of the property.

Women's negotiating strengths

Step 1: make them trust you

From the moment we are born, we trust our mothers for survival. This lingers on throughout our life. In times of trouble where possible, we turn to Mom. For this reason, motherhood or the female represents trust and problem solving.

Remember that motivated sellers are often selling because they are in trouble of some kind. For you to help them the most, you need them to trust you. Women are seen as more trustworthy than men, so build on this.

Avoid intimidation

Homeowners are less intimidated by women – especially when the seller is a woman. Here are some strategies to make people feel less intimidated and more comfortable:

If possible, meet in the kitchen. Have you ever noticed that during parties, everyone seems to gather in the kitchen? This room is a symbol of family and sharing. Plus, the kitchen often has a table which makes it easier for you to write notes and sign contracts.

If possible, sit diagonally (kitty-corner) from each other to create a feeling of empathy or partnership. Sitting across from each other is more intimidating.

If they offer you a cup of coffee or a glass of water, accept it. Even if you don't drink from the glass, you have accepted their hospitality and have accepted them and their situation.

Sit on their furniture when invited. Even if you consider the house to be unkempt or dirty you do not want to offend the homeowner.

Ask them to turn off the television or the radio. You can say something like: "Could you please turn off the television. I am getting distracted and I really want to hear what you have to say." This lets the homeowner know you care about their input. It also puts you in control of the situation. You are getting their attention.

Put the homeowner on your level. Use their language and their colloquialisms to show you and they are more alike than different.

Be interested in them

It has been said that the seller is not interested in selling to you until they believe you are interested in them.

Ask questions. Let them talk as long as they need to, especially when you are buying from an older person. They need to talk.

As they are talking:

- ⇢ Listen to the words they use
- ⇢ Watch their body language
- ⇢ Write down the names of children, grandchildren, pets, and favorite sports teams
- ⇢ Look around their home or office to notice their hobbies or types of books they read
- ⇢ Determine what they are concerned about

When you are done, you will have all the information you need to start a successful negotiation.

Create affinity

People like to do business with people they like.

After all your questions, you will certainly find some things you have in common. Maybe you both like the same sports team or can talk about kids or hobbies. You may even have some friends in common.

This part of the conversation may take five to fifteen minutes. It's short but very important. This will create the foundation of your relationship going forward.

Dress like they dress

To have someone trust you, you want to dress a certain way. You want to show respect by dressing one step better than they are dressed. However, in my opinion you do not want to overdress. This will require you to be familiar with your clients. If they are used to dressing in their Sunday best with dresses and suits then you should dress similarly. However, if they tend to wear jeans and flannel shirts, you might want to wear a simple dress or slacks with a nice top. Always wear comfortable shoes if you are going to be walking the property.

Step 2: get them to open up to you to uncover their challenge

When you are speaking to a motivated seller, it is very important to find out why they are selling. Some people are very open and will share all the details you are interested in (and more!). They will talk for as long as you let them.

Other people are more reserved. You will need to ask probing questions in a polite manner so you can uncover what is really bothering them.

Ask the same question in different ways

Remember you will have to ask the same question in differing ways. People will tell you more details about their situation as they trust you more and more. It is not that they want to lie; it's more that they may be embarrassed about their situation.

For example, you could ask:

Why do you want to move? *I don't need this big house anymore.*

Do you need to move? *To tell you the truth, I can't afford the taxes anymore.*

When you sell your house (or rental property), what are you going to do next? *I really want to move in with my family in another state.*

All of these questions are similar. However, they may get you different answers. Obviously, do not ask these questions back to back. Intersperse them with other questions.

Visit the property and the seller several times

Think about this: When you shopped for a new home and you found one you liked, didn't you walk through it a couple of times before making an offer?

Then why do we feel this pressure to make an offer immediately upon walking through the property? Each time you visit you will see new features/challenges with the property and you will build a stronger rapport. I have found you can get lower pricing and better terms if you can meet with the seller several times. (You can do these multiple visits in the span of forty-eight hours if you want to move quickly.)

Step 3: make an offer

You CANNOT buy a property without making an offer.

I know that this sounds obvious but it needs to be said.

Go ahead – make an offer.

They will say yes, no or counter-offer.

Too many people I know will do Steps 1 and 2 very well. Then they go home to analyze the deal. They spend two weeks analyzing the repair costs and another two weeks figuring out what the property is worth. Then they hem and haw for another week. They are struck with paralysis by analysis.

A husband and wife team, found a property they wanted to rehab. It was on the Multiple Listing Service as a bank-owned (REO) property. He comes from the construction industry but he still took weeks to send in his offer. The bank came back and wanted a higher offer. They took almost a week to submit another offer. By then the property was sold to another person!

Analyze the deal within seventy-two hours (or less) and make an offer. Keep following up until you get the property or someone else does!

Go to a flea market

Americans think the price is the price. Automobiles are the only exception for some reason. We expect to negotiate over the price of a car but not anything else we find in a store.

A century ago (and in many parts of the world today), we would do our grocery shopping at the local outdoor market. The farmers brought in the fruits and vegetables, fishmongers would bring in the daily catch, and meat would come from the farm. We would buy food every day or every other day. And there would be a lot of bargaining going on.

Today we have flea markets, tag sales, estate sales, and garage sales. In your town you might have a farmer's market, auction house, or antique sale. Online, we have Craigslist as well as eBay and other auction sites.

So now I want you to practice negotiating by going to a flea market (or one of the places I just mentioned) this weekend and buy something for 10 cents on the dollar. That's correct. I want you to pay 10 cents for something that is priced at one dollar.

"But Linda", you are thinking, "how is buying a mug for 10 cents (instead of $1) going to help me buy a house that is

$100,000?" Because I believe that success breeds success. When you have success paying 10% of the original price on a mug, your brain emits endorphins and you are happy. The brain will emit the same endorphins when you have success with a much bigger number. In other words, one dollar means as much as $100,000.

Here is the other reason I want you to do this. As a salesperson, I have found it is much easier to make a sale when I don't care whether I make the sale or not. If I don't care, I can stay loose and relaxed. I can stay focused on the other person, figure out what they really want, and create an offer that works for both of us.

Do you really care whether or not you buy that mug? No, of course not. You can just walk away. Let the seller come after you to make an offer.

Right after high school, I lived in Israel for nine months. While living in Jerusalem, I often went to the souk (market). There you could buy spices, fish, vegetables, scarves, rugs, everything. Everyone bargains for everything. As an American, I had never seen anything like it. One day I saw a blouse I really liked. So I thought I would try my skill at bargaining. (Keep in mind this happened forty years ago so the numbers are not accurate but you will get the point.)

Let's say the tag said 100 agorot (1 shekel)

I made an offer of 45 agorot.

The salesman flinched and started telling me about all the wonderful features of the blouse: beautiful embroidery, soft material, lovely color. He also told me how beautiful it looked on me.

Then he said: "The lowest I can go is 90 agorot." That is 10% off!

So then I offered 55 agorot.

After a couple more negotiations, I was still not satisfied.

I started to walk away.

And then he said the magic words to my back: "Pretty lady, how about 65 agorot?"

I went back slowly and bought the blouse which I wore proudly for several years. I saved 35% just by talking, not caring too much, walking away, and then saying yes!

Now it is your turn. Go to a market this weekend. Find something you want to buy and negotiate your price. Practice negotiating and have fun with it.

BONUS: Make money with the item you just bought. Put it on Craigslist or eBay and sell it for more than you paid for it Congratulations! You're now a wholesaler!

EXTRA BONUS: Send me an email and share your story with me. I love hearing the bargains my students get. In the book *Women are Just Better at Selling and Negotiating*, I will share all kinds of negotiating strategies that will save you money and get you better terms on real estate deals.

Networking

A.k.a the Old Girls' Club

I was talking to my student Liz earlier. I hadn't spoken to her in a month and I wanted to make sure she was still on the path to success.

"Great news!" she said. "I just added three contracts to my cleaning business in just one month!"

"Congratulations! Does this mean that you just doubled your business?"

"Yep!" she said proudly.

"So how did you do it? What made the difference?"

"Word of mouth" she said. "I have been attending networking meetings of all kinds … real estate investing groups, the Chamber of Commerce, Business Networking International… everyone knows who I am!"

The Old Boys' Club

You have probably heard of the *Old Boys' Club*. Back room deals made in cigar smoke-filled bars and men's only clubs. There is a reason why US Presidents and world leaders are always seen playing golf. Away from telephones and computers, in a relaxed atmosphere, handshake deals are easy to make.

> The Royal Ancient Golf Club of Scotland only admitted women members in 2014.

> The Augusta National Golf Club in Augusta, Georgia USA didn't accept women members until 2012.

> In 2016, the Muirfield Golf Course in Scotland voted to continue banning women from membership. As a result, they were banned from hosting a British Open.

Since women (and minorities) were excluded from these clubs men had the advantage for negotiating deals in an informal setting. Business mergers, land deals, political appointments and real estate developments have all been initiated in "men only" establishments.

Creating the Old Girls' Club

Despite this disadvantage (or maybe because of it), women have figured out a way to create our own Old Girls' Club. We get together for playdates with our children and we organize coffee klatches with our neighbors. We attend sisterhood meetings at our church/synagogue/mosque and show up for dinner meetings at women's business associations. We meet our friends for book group discussions or tennis matches or scrapbooking. We are social human beings, getting together for gossip, exchanging ideas, and companionship. We come together in times of joy and of sorrow. We are always ready to bring a dinner to a grieving family or cookies to a celebration.

Our ability to create strong, deep, and abiding relationships pays off when it really counts. In 2013, congresswomen crossed party lines to create a way to reopen the U.S. government after it shut down over congressional partisan budgetary disagreements. *Time* magazine commented:

> It's quite an irony that the U.S. Senate was once known for having the worst vestiges of a private men's club: unspoken rules, hidden alliances, off-hours socializing and an ethic based at least as much on personal relationships as merit to get things done. That Senate — a fraternal paradise that worked despite all its obvious shortcomings — is long gone. And now the only place the old boys' network seems to function anymore is among the four Republicans and 16 Democrats who happen to be women.[20]

Women are better at developing relationships and rapport than are men

According to the Relationship Institute located in Michigan, women are different than men when it comes to relationships. Women value love, communication, beauty and relationships.

> A woman's sense of self is defined through their feelings and the quality of their relationships. They spend much time supporting, nurturing and helping each other. They experience fulfillment through sharing and relating.

> Communication is important. Talking, sharing and relating is how a woman feels good about herself.

> For women, offering help is not a sign of weakness but a sign of strength; it is a sign of caring to give support.[21]

20 Newton-Small, Jay, "Women Are the Only Adults Left in Washington", *Time Magazine*, October 16 2013, swampland.time.com/2013/10/16/women-are-the-only-adults-left-in-washington (accessed July 16 2016).
21 "Differences Between Men and Women", Relationship Institute, January

Does this sound true for you?

Women tend to have higher emotional intelligence (EQ) than men, especially in the area of empathy. On the other hand, men are better at compartmentalizing their emotions. Peter Salovey and John D. Mayer first coined the term 'Emotional Intelligence' in 1990 describing it as "a form of social intelligence that involves the ability to monitor one's own and others' feelings and emotions, to discriminate among them, and to use this information to guide one's thinking and action".[22]

In 1995, Daniel Goleman Ph.D. wrote the New York Times bestseller Emotional Intelligence and Social Intelligence: The New Science of Human Relationships. Goleman proposed that EQ is more important than IQ as a predictor of being successful in life. Goleman says:

> Emotional intelligence has four parts: self-awareness, managing our emotions, empathy, and social skills. There are many tests of emotional intelligence, and most seem to show that women tend to have an edge over men when it comes to these basic skills for a happy and successful life. That edge may matter more than ever in the workplace, as more companies are starting to recognize the advantages of high EI when it comes to positions like sales, teams, and leadership.
>
> On the other hand, it's not that simple. For instance, some measures suggest women are on average better than men at some forms of empathy, and men do better than women when it comes to managing distressing emotions.
>
> Women tend to be better at emotional empathy than

15 2015 relationship-institute.com/differences-between-men-and-women/ (accessed July 17 2016).

22 Golis, Chris, "A Brief History of Emotional Intelligence", Practical Emotional Intelligence, www.emotionalintelligencecourse.com/eq-history (accessed July 17 2016).

men, in general. This kind of empathy fosters rapport and chemistry. People who excel in emotional empathy make good counselors, teachers, and group leaders because of this ability to sense in the moment how others are reacting.

Here's where women differ from men. If the other person is upset, or the emotions are disturbing, women's brains tend to stay with those feelings. But men's brains do something else: they sense the feelings for a moment, then tune out of the emotions and switch to other brain areas that try to solve the problem that's creating the disturbance.

Neither is better—both have advantages. The male tune-out works well when there's a need to insulate yourself against distress so you can stay calm while others around you are falling apart—and focus on finding a solution to an urgent problem. And the female tendency to stay tuned in helps enormously to nurture and support others in emotionally trying circumstances.[23]

For example, when meeting with a family who is going through foreclosure proceedings, a woman may naturally be more effective at building rapport and expressing empathy for the family's struggles. However, a woman also may get too involved in the sympathy instead of creating a solution that can help the family let go of their house and find peace in the future with a new place to live.

The good news is that you can develop the skills of emotional intelligence once you discover where you are in the spectrum of EQ.

---

23 Goleman, Daniel, "Are Women More Emotionally Intelligent than Men?" May 6 2011 www.danielgoleman.info/are-women-more-emotionally-intelligent-than-men (accessed July 16 2016)

Women make business deals through relationships

Women tend to be more relational whereas men are more transactional. Women are willing, and in fact prefer, to build the relationship first and then ask for the sale.

Many of my students come to me after having been taught to submit hundreds of low-ball offers at a time. In fact, they have been taught that if you are not embarrassed to submit the offer, it is not low enough. Now this strategy certainly does work, but it comes with a whole heap of rejection and anger too. Sellers and real estate agents are annoyed and insulted. They refuse to deal. The students come to me frustrated that their offers are not being accepted. They feel like they are wasting their time and money.

The secret is that you can buy properties at those low-ball prices without annoying the seller. If you are willing to take a little time to build rapport with the seller, you will find that you will buy more properties at deep discounts and favorable terms.

One of my students found a property while driving her neighborhood. The little house was on a beautiful riverside property, had some updates and needed some work. Two brothers were selling it and they each had different reasons to sell and different prices in mind! One was local so he was stuck with the maintenance responsibilities. The other lived out of state and thought he was sitting on a gold mine. She had multiple conversations with each brother, finding their personality, needs, and priorities. This investment paid off beautifully. She bought the house for $20,000 less than asking price, and negotiated the terms of her purchase, asking if she could make monthly payments of $319 for a year. They accepted but wanted $5000 down. After a few more conversations, she bought the house without bringing one dollar to the closing table! Wasn't it worth it to her to build rapport first?

Why is networking important in real estate (and why must you learn how to do it)?

You can find the best deals, the lowest prices and most flexible terms when you are dealing with off-market properties. You do not have any competition and so you have time to negotiate the best deal for you and for the seller. The best way to find off-market deals is through the relationships you create through networking.

You are looking for motivated sellers. If you are looking and listening, you will find that someone in your circle of friends needs to sell their home or their property. Every day someone unfortunately finds themselves in a predicament and needs someone they trust to create a solution. Think about it. If you were going through a divorce or job loss and you needed to sell your house, you would want to work with someone who could handle the situation discretely. You don't want to advertise your situation by going on the MLS. You certainly don't want to see your name on public record as you go through the foreclosure process.

When you are networking with people and socializing with people, you become the person they trust. You become the go-to person to solve their situation. By nature networking is social and informal. Networking is more than just handing over a business card.

Where should you go to meet people?

Maybe a better question is where shouldn't you go? You can meet people everywhere. Here are just a few ideas:

→ Business organizations: Chamber of Commerce, Business Network International, your local real estate investor association, your local landlord association

→ Service organizations: Rotary, Elks, Freemasons, etc.

→ School groups your children are involved in: Parent teacher organizations, sports teams, Girl and Boy Scouts

→ Hobbies: ballroom dancing, stamp collecting, gardening, flower arranging, chess, orchestras, skiing, tennis, boating, golf.

→ Your neighborhood, beach, or condo association

→ Your religious group

→ Political organizations: it doesn't matter which party you belong to; it only matters that you meet people you can relate to. You may want to be appointed to the planning and zoning variance committee or other local government boards that impact real estate in your area.

→ Meetup groups: go to www.Meetup.com and sign up for groups that match your interests.

→ Volunteer for non-profit organizations in your area; attend fundraisers or help organize them; join the board of directors for a non-profit organization.

The list goes on. The important thing is that you are meeting people and they are meeting you. By the way, I recommend volunteering for whatever group you are part of. It doesn't have to take up a lot of time, depending on the role you volunteer for. When you are a volunteer, you are more visible and people think you know something (even if it is your first day on the post!) New people are more likely to start a conversation with you and so will the old-timers. Many times volunteering allows you to attend paid functions, like fundraisers, for free.

Be the only person in the crowd

My partner and I foster dogs and cats. The faster we can find homes for each animal, the more animals we can save. So we often pack up the cats and the dogs and take them to one of the animal big box stores. Alternatively, we post them on Petfinder.com. This sounds logical; however, almost everyone walking through the store already has a pet and is not looking for another one. Sometimes we are much more successful when we list the pet on Craigslist or on Facebook or set up a booth in store that is not a pet store. We put our product in a place where there is very little competition. (Of course, we screen all applicants very carefully.)

I sold health insurance for nine years. One of the best places for me to get leads was to set up a table at a country fair! You might say, "Why would you want to hang out with the cows and the pigs and the chickens to sell health insurance?" The answer is that I was the ONLY one selling health insurance at such a fair. Farmers need health insurance and so do the thousands of families who attend the fairs. Since I was the only one there, I cornered the market and usually walked away with a hundred leads in one weekend.

Similarly, although I go to many business-oriented networking meetings, sometimes I have much more success by going somewhere that has nothing to do with real estate or with business. For example, one of my students is a ballroom dancer and she attends ballroom dances. I suggested she create business cards that say "Ballroom Dancer Buys Houses" and put her picture on it. This slogan is memorable, plus if one of her dancing friends needs to sell their house, they know they have something in common with her.

What's in a business card?

Speaking of business cards, how do you handle them? Throw them in a drawer and forget about them? Or maybe you enter them into your data base and once in a while send out an email blast? Or maybe you actually call the person only to blab about yourself?

In my work with real estate investors, I had the opportunity to go to the United States Capitol to do some lobbying. While there, one of the senator's staffers explained how the Japanese exchange business cards. He said that the Japanese person receiving your business card puts the card in both of her hands and gives a slight bow. This gives reverence to the card as much as she gives reverence to you. The person receiving your card considers the card to be a full representation of you.

What if you treated each business card as a representation of the person? How would you treat each card then?

How to network

Although women are naturally more social, not all of us are comfortable in networking situations. I myself am very shy by nature. I needed to teach myself how to network. Without networking, I would not have been able to put food on my table as an insurance agent!

So here are some helpful hints that have worked for me.

She is just as afraid of you as you are of her

Have you ever attended a networking meeting? Have you noticed that all the bank people stand together and all the car dealer people stand together? This is a networking event. Why do they hang out with people they work with every day? Why aren't they meeting new people?

Because they are afraid to meet new people. That's right. The people attending the networking event are as nervous of meeting YOU as you are of them!

Meet someone in the first five minutes of arriving

How did I conquer my fear? I force myself to meet someone new within the first five minutes of arriving at the event. I may walk up to someone who is standing by themselves, or I may wiggle myself into the small crowd of co-workers.

Either way, I make sure I meet someone in the first five minutes. If I wait longer than that, my fears get ahead of me and I have defeated the purpose of attending. By the way, this strategy works at parties and all sorts of other gatherings.

Meet the organizer – ask her to introduce you to people

The job of the organizer (or president or board member) is to serve the attendees. She wants people to get the most value out of the program so that they attend again. If it is a business group, her role is to help attendees create more business.

Let her know the type of person you are looking to meet and ask her to introduce you to them. An introduction from her will open up plenty of doors for you. Even if she only points out people to meet, you could say, "The organizer suggested we had something in common and we should meet."

Meet the keynote speaker – ask her to introduce you to people

The keynote speaker already has social influence with the people attending. After all, her name and credentials have probably been posted on all of the postcards, emails, and newsletters promoting the event.

I recommend you walk up to her and ask her a question like, How can I refer business to you?" or "Is there a company you would like to be introduced to?" or "How can I help you?"

Then she will naturally ask you similar questions and can help introduce you to people in the room.

Immediately after the meeting, send her a referral or some helpful information. She will most likely return the favor in kind.

Be more interested in them

The natural tendency at these meetings is to think you have a very short time period to get your message across. You run around to as many people as possible, spilling out your thirty second commercial and grabbing business cards. At the end of the meeting, you have no idea who you met and you can't remember which business card goes with each human being.

First of all, the nice thing about joining organizations especially networking organizations, is that you will see many of the same people over and over again. This helps you build long term relationships. This is especially important in our industry because you never know when someone's circumstances put them in a situation where they need to sell their property.

Be more interested in the other person. Ask them about their business and their family. Especially at a business function ask them questions like:

> *Who would be your perfect customer?*
>
> *Are you trying to meet a specific person or a specific company?*
>
> *Are you having any challenges you need help with?*
> *Do you see any specific opportunities I can help you with?*
>
> *What makes you unique or different from your other competitors?*

If you can, see if you can find something in common with them. This is easy if you are meeting them at an affinity group (e.g. you have children, beliefs or hobbies in common).

Follow up, follow up, follow up

Have you ever heard the phrase "the money is in the follow up?" Most people think that all they need to do is go to the meeting, hand out their card, and wait for people to call them. This is rarely the case. Unless you reach out to the prospect, you will rarely make any money.

What you do next will differentiate you from all the others. Right after the meeting, organize your business cards to identify people you want to connect with immediately and those you want to add to your contact list.

Refer to your notes on each card. Hopefully, you can make a referral or find an interesting article for each lead. Call up the person and schedule coffee with them. Bring your referral with you. The Law of Reciprocity says that your new contact will want to repay you for the attention you bring them.

Schedule three or four informal meetings a week. Then follow up with a thank you note, a weekly email and a phone call. If you are able to provide value for the other person, you will become their go-to person to solve real estate challenges.

Your 30-second elevator speech

You definitely want to have a thirty-second elevator speech prepared so you can share your business quickly and precisely. There are many books about this subject. Indeed, many leads groups will train you on how to put together your statement. Here are some key points to include:

- ⤙ What service you provide
- ⤙ Who your target customers are
- ⤙ How you are unique from others
- ⤙ Why people want to do business with you

For example:

> *I help homeowners and landlords solve their real estate problems. If possible, I help them stay in their property. However, if they discover they need to sell, I buy the property for a fair price and help them move on with their lives. Do you know someone who can't afford to pay their mortgage or who has inherited a house or is tired of being a landlord?*

I like ending my speech with a question. People naturally need to answer questions to close the loop in their brain. They also like to be helpful. They will usually answer:

> "No, I don't know anyone like that right now. Do you have a card so that I can keep you in mind?"

-or-

> "I think you should meet so-and-so. I would be happy to make the introduction."

Follow up, follow up, follow up: Part 2

How do you follow up? Do you use email, letters, postcards or social media?

I recommend you send an email to people on your list at least once a week so they remember you. In other words, you want to have top of mind awareness whenever they, or their friends, need you.

What should you say in your follow up? You could:

➤ Share interesting articles about real estate in your area

➤ Share information about your real estate activities

➤ Give progress reports about properties you are rehabbing

➤ Tell funny stories about contractors, tenants, dogs, kids and more

➤ Give them helpful hints, e.g., spring cleaning, preparing for winter

Now how can you possibly do this in your busy life? Here are some resources to automate this process as much as possible:

➤ Use an autoresponder to send out emails to your list. Constant Contact, ChimpMail, and BigMoneyCart are some popular companies. Autoresponders allow you to set up a series of emails up front. When you add a new person, you can automatically send out emails every couple of days.

➤ Use a service like SendOut Cards to upload your mailing list and mail real letters. You could even include gift cards. As with autoresponders, you can set up a series of cards or letters and the system will send them automatically on the day you want them sent out.

Where are the best deals?

E VERY REAL ESTATE AGENT I KNOW has heard this from a new client: "I want to buy a deal. I want to buy something at 50% off so I can fix it up and sell it for big bucks. Could you find me a deal?"

Sounds reasonable, right?

WRONG.

There are no deals

There are no deals?

That's right.

There are no deals served to you on a silver platter. Sure, every once in a while, you might find a "perfect" deal. But by the time you hear about it, there are many other offers and the price is above what you are willing to pay for it.

There are certainly "dogs": deals that have been hanging around the MLS for 180 days, 365 days, even 270 days! As my partner always said to me: "If it was such a good deal it would have been sold already." Of course, this is a self-fulfilling prophecy ensuring failure. This sentence really predicts that you can never find a good deal.

There are only deals that you create

The truth of the matter is that the only good deals are the deals you create.

That's right – your ability to make money in real estate is totally predicated on your ability to create the transaction. The deal you create will have the following features:

- ➤ The right location
- ➤ The right property
- ➤ The right rehab cost
- ➤ The right value-add feature
- ➤ The right purchase price
- ➤ The right terms
- ➤ The right cash flow
- ➤ The right sales price

Wow! Sounds complicated, right? Not really. Much of this is common sense and skills you already have. I love to show people like you how to convert your life skills into successful real estate profits. The rest of the deal-making skills can be taught. You will learn them in *Women are Simply Better at Getting Started in Real Estate*.

The best deals are the ones you find yourself

Every day I hear real estate investors complain to me, "I can't find any deals."

When I ask them where they are looking, they tell me, "On the MLS."

"That's the problem, " I tell them.

When I first started investing in real estate, the only way I could find out what properties were for sale was to go into my real estate agent's office. In her office, she had book after book after book of listings. And we would page through each book until we found the properties we were interested in.

Now, however, it's a totally different story. Just fire up your computer, tablet or smartphone, and you can see everything for sale with a swipe of a finger.

Convenient, yes. But it also means everyone else on the planet can see the same properties you can. And everyone else can make offers, which means you have lots of competition. This gets worse in hot markets where you are competing with both investors and potential homeowners who are willing to buy handywomen specials.

Think outside the box to find off-market deals

So what's the smart real estate entrepreneur to do?

Go out and find real estate deals no one else know about.

Where are these deals you say?

They are right in front of your nose – or in your network.

The motivated seller

The best deals are going to come from someone who is motivated to sell. By motivated we mean someone who needs to sell or who really wants to sell. For example, your neighbor may tell you she wants to sell her house because she is looking to move to a bigger house. She just painted the house inside and out, and she replaced the roof. By the way, she upgraded her kitchen and her master bathroom last year.

When you ask her how much she wants, she tells you she wants $10,000 more than her neighbor got for his house last summer. By the way, her house is bigger and her gardens are nicer.

Your neighbor is NOT motivated. Although she wants to sell, she can afford to sit around and wait until she gets the price she wants. The best thing to do here is to refer her to your favorite real estate agent. Your real estate agent may be able to reciprocate the favor someday and you will be the first person your neighbor calls to thank you for helping her sell the house. She will also call you when she finds out her property is not worth what she thinks it is worth and she wants you to buy it from her at a much more reasonable price.

A motivated seller is someone who has a motive for selling. Just like in your favorite murder-mystery where the detective is looking to discover the person's real motive for killing, you are looking for the person's real motive for selling.

A motivated seller is someone who needs to sell or really, really, really wants to sell. A motivated seller will be willing to sell you their property for a discount or on creative terms. She will want to sell very quickly. This allows you to increase your profits.

Why would someone be motivated to sell?

Think about this for a moment and you will come up with a variety of reasons. Perhaps:

> ➤ She is going through a divorce and cannot afford to keep the home, or maybe the court is mandating that the house be sold.

> ➤ She lost her job or had some unexpected medical bills and can no longer afford the house.

> ➤ She is a landlady who is tired of being a landlord. Unfortunately, many property owners do not get trained on how to screen tenants and how to manage properties. They often find themselves at eviction court, making expensive repairs, or having too many vacancies.

> ➤ She may be ready to retire and doesn't want to be an active investor anymore. However, she can't pay the capital gains tax due on the building and is looking for a way out.

> ➤ She is older and on a fixed income. She cannot afford the property taxes or the mortgage payments on her home anymore.

➢ She is being transferred or getting married, and can't afford to pay two mortgages on two houses.

➢ Her relative passed away and left her the house. Now she needs to sell it but lives far away; or she just doesn't want to keep the rental property.

Why does a motivated seller need you?

Maybe you have been in one of these situations yourself or maybe you know someone who has. You know that these situations are private. Often, people lose sleep over them. They withdraw from others. They don't want anyone to know the pain they are going through.

A motivated seller needs someone to confide in, someone they can trust to keep confidences and who can come up with solutions that really work.

Unfortunately, so many people have faced job loss that it is not so embarrassing any more to go through foreclosure. They may put up a brave face and say the bank is the one who did them wrong. Don't be fooled. These are middle class and wealthy people who were living the American dream. Oftentimes, they were the first person in their family to own their own home. Foreclosure is devastating for everyone.

As a woman, you can bring compassion and understanding to a tough situation. You may even build trust by sharing your own experience. And then you can be the one who offers them the solution they have been looking for.

Once you build rapport, they will trust your solution as being one that brings them peace of mind and allows them to move forward with their life.

Peace of mind – not price

Notice that I did not say you would bring them the best price for their property. I said that your solution would bring them peace of mind.

> One time we got a phone call from an elderly woman who wanted to sell her three-family house. She had met us when we bought her neighbor's house. Eleanor and her family had lived in this house for eighty years ever since they arrived in America from Italy!
>
> Her brother had just passed away and she was ready to move to assisted living with her sister. She was very proud of her house. She told us she would clear out all of the furniture and all of the odds and ends accumulated from living in a place of eighty years.
>
> We assured her that she did not need to move anything. We would take care of it all. (One of the benefits of buying houses is getting lots of quality items for free!)
>
> She trusted us to take care of her house the way her family had taken care of it and to take care of her the way we had taken care of the neighbor. She did not want to list it with a real estate agent and face uncertainty of when the property would sell. She simply wanted to move on to her new home.
>
> Could she have gotten a higher price if she'd cleaned out the three apartments, painted them, made repairs and listed it with a real estate agent? Maybe. Instead she got a fair price from us. We were able to buy it at a discount, turn it around quickly, and generate strong cash flow. As a bonus, we were able to sell it a few years later for a hefty profit.

Did you know that banks can be motivated sellers?

Some of the most motivated of all motivated sellers can be banks. For each mortgage, the bank needs to keep a percentage in reserve. When the borrower doesn't pay the mortgage, the bank needs to sell the property so that its reserves are replenished.

If you can make an offer that the bank (and its investors) can accept, the bank will sell you the property for much less than the original face value of the mortgage/note. Before foreclosure, this is called selling the property as a "short sale" (selling for less than the face value of the mortgage). After the foreclosure, you are buying a REO (real estate owned) property.

Since the banks require that the property be listed on the MLS before accepting a short sale, I recommend you find a real estate agent well-trained in the art of REO and short sale negotiation. I also recommend that you study the foreclosure laws in your state. This is public information and often available for free. You may physically need to go to the courthouse handling foreclosures (county or state). Most states have this information on their website.

How do you reach these motivated sellers?

Now that you know about motivated sellers, the big question is how do you reach them? Also, how can they find about you so that they will reach out to you?

Direct mail is the key

When was the last time you received a letter in the mail? Think hard now.

Perhaps a birthday card?
An invitation to a party?
A thank you note for a gift you gave?
Maybe a Christmas card ... enclosed with a typed letter where your friend brags about all of the accomplishments of her family?

And that's about it. Long letters to friends have been replaced with email and Facebook.

So imagine if you received a letter in an invitation envelope with a handwritten address, creative stamp and a personal return address.

Would you throw it away? Or open it right away?

Almost everyone receiving such an envelope would be curious enough to tear it open and read it.

In fact, if you do it right, you can get up to 30% response to your mail. This is in big contrast to much direct mail which only gets a 1-3% response rate.

Even the big companies are sending mail

Direct mail is even being used by Google!

That's right – the internet giant uses direct mail to acquire new customers! Every few months, I receive an invitation with a coupon code from Google to entice me to buy advertising from them. If it works for Google, who are we to argue?

The advantage of mail

Mail has a lot of advantages:

➤ People hold onto mail until the time they need to contact you.

➤ You can send mail specifically to someone who might be interested in your offer (as opposed to hoping that someone seeing your billboard would be interested in your offer).

➤ A letter is personal. Your letter can be written specifically to one person who you believe wants to meet you. Or your letter can be more generic while explaining the services you offer.

➤ Mail is relatively inexpensive compared to radio, television, and internet ads.

➤ You can send an informational report. You can also send gift cards, funny cartoons, or other items to build rapport.

➤ A letter is not as intrusive as a phone call or conversation.

o Have you ever gone into a store to buy an outfit, and the sales clerk asks: "Can I help you?" If you are like most people, your automatic knee jerk reaction is to say "no" even though you really need her assistance to find that perfect ensemble for your cousin's soiree.

o When someone who is facing foreclosure receives your letter, they are desperate for your help. However, she is very likely to hang up the phone on you before you can even explain your services. She may not even pick up the phone because she is avoiding all creditors.

o The beauty of sending a letter or even a postcard is that the reader the reader can consider your message before automatically turning you down.

Why women are better suited to using direct mail

Direct mail is perfect for women to use. By its very nature, letters are designed to convey a message and to create a relationship. In a letter, you can introduce yourself to the reader. You can convey empathy to the reader and the reader's situation. This plays to women's strengths.

Pencraft

Think about the last card or letter you received.

Think about the writing on the envelope or inside the card.

Could you tell the difference between a man/boy's writing or a girl/woman's writing?

In general, women's handwriting is more open, friendlier, and creates more trust.

I have been teaching about direct mail for a number of years. A student of mine, let's call him Rob, complained to me that he had followed all of my instructions and yet he did not receive any results. So I asked him to show me what he was sending.

As soon as I saw his envelope and letter, I knew exactly what had happened.

Rob's a guy with a guy's handwriting. The writing on the letters was sloppy and leaned to the left. His letter didn't generate feelings of good will and trust.

Then I called on another student, let's call her Jane, to show us her mailers. Her handwriting was round and friendly, on personal stationery with a handwritten envelope and letter. She had received many more responses than Rob.

It became clear that presentation makes all of the difference. Your letter or postcard is the only way your prospect initially knows who you are. If the recipient feels she can trust you or that you can solve their problem, she will pick up the phone and call you. If she thinks the letter is sloppy or not professional, she may ignore it and throw it in the trash.

Other ways to find deals

You have many other ways of finding deals. Phone calls, running ads in the newspaper and online, putting up yard signs, and sending emails to your associates are just a few. With all of these methods, I believe that women can use their relationship building skills and presentation skills to a great advantage over men.

Women know what women want

Women buy the house: men (or women) pay for it

Real estate agents are in the business of selling houses. Over time they develop a sixth sense enabling them to know what buyers really want (not just what they say they want.)

So walk up to a successful real estate agent and pose this question:

"If a husband and wife are buying a house, who chooses the home they are buying?"

I guarantee they will say, "Women buy the house."

Then go ahead and ask her one more question:

"What are women looking for in a house? What are the most important rooms?"

And again I guarantee they will say: "The bathroom and the kitchen."

Rehab the house (or apartment) to sell (or rent)

Elsewhere in this book we discussed how important it is to have more than one exit strategy. This will help you avoid being stuck with a house that cannot sell or rent.

Similarly, from Day 1, you want to renovate the property with your end goal in mind: rent or sell.

If the kitchen and bathrooms are not desirable, you will have a tough time selling your property. If the woman thinks the bathroom is too small or ugly, if she cannot reach the kitchen cabinets or doesn't like the kitchen layout, you are not going to sell the house. Period.

Of course, adding a "she shed" (like a "man cave") and a nice garage will seal the deal.

Holding costs

Each day you hold onto a property, it costs you money. We call this "holding costs". Think about it for a moment and you will know what I mean. What do you have to pay for each and every day while you are rehabbing or holding a property?

→ The cost of money (this could be a bank mortgage, hard money loan, or borrowing from someone you know).

→ Property taxes

→ Insurance

→ Utilities

→ Heat or air conditioning. This can be HUGE, depending on the time of year. In fact, many rehabbers in the Northeast USA do everything they can to avoid holding houses during the winter months.

→ Mowing the lawn, shoveling snow and landscaping

When investors calculate their profit in a property, they remember to account for purchase price, selling price rehabbing costs and real estate agent commission. However they often forget to calculate these holding costs.

- ⇥ Six to eight weeks to rehab
- ⇥ Two months to find a buyer (ask your real estate agent for the typical "days on market" for your location)
- ⇥ One to two months to have the mortgage approved and to close the sale

THEN if the buyer falls through, you have to repeat the process and before you know it, six more months have passed.

Now, take all of the costs listed above and you can calculate the nine-month holding costs involved.

If you REALLY want to be motivated to get your project done on time and under budget, figure out how much your property costs you EACH DAY you hold it. Say you figure out that the property costs you $100 a day. That's like burning a $100 bill each day!

Now use all of your skills to get that property fixed up and sold or rented as quickly as possible!

Recommendation: Create a thermometer showing your daily holding costs and post it where you can see it every day. This will help you stay focused on the end result.

Women know what other women want

As women, we understand women better than men. So as real estate investors we have an advantage over men.

We are more likely to understand design and color.

Also, we are more likely to stay current as desires change.

We spend a lot of time in the kitchen preparing meals for ourselves and our family. We have often cursed the "man" who designed this kitchen or who put the cabinets up too high!

If only a woman would have designed this _____, we wouldn't be having this challenge.

And we certainly spend a lot of time in the bathroom!

Even if you don't have an eye for design, you can do the research

Even if you do not understand design, you have many resources at your fingertips.

Normally, I would tell you to turn off your television to focus on achieving your goals. However, I have invested hours of time watching TV shows. Study these shows to find out what people want. You will discover the current trends in color and design. These shows also help you see possibilities that you wouldn't discover otherwise.

NOTE: The biggest challenge most people have is that they cannot see beyond the smell, trash, poor design, mold and more. Your profits are a direct correlation of your ability to see the possibility of the property without breaking the bank!

For example, you will see how you can open up a room by removing a full wall or half wall.

You will discover how to use color to brighten up a room or give the impression that the house is bigger or cozier, depending on what you need.

In essence, you will see so many reveals and so many before/after pictures, you are training yourself to envision the after when you are buying the before picture.

Record these shows so you can really study them. Soon you will automatically see options for the properties you are buying.

Design and rehab with the end goal in mind

Your goal is to make a profit, correct?

I have seen many contractors, builders, designers, and women who "love to do interior decorating" fail at the buy/fix/sell game. These professionals are used to doing custom work. They have one customer they need to please. They get to know their client. They understand their client's taste, desires, and budget. Then they do the job they are asked to do.

When you are rehabbing a house for a quick sell, you do not know the exact person or family who is going to buy the house. If you create a custom one-of-a-kind house, you have severely limited the number of buyers for your house.

There is a big difference between renovating a property for your own personal taste versus renovating a property to appeal to your buyers. Have you ever seen out-takes of renovating shows where the owner is appalled with the result? They may be humorous for television but this is the exact opposite of the result you are hoping to achieve.

Think of your property as a neutral blank canvas. Ideally, you want your buyer to envision their furniture, their photographs and pictures, their kids' toys and their big screen TV inside of this canvas.

So yes, I recommend you stage the finished product with furniture and pictures. However, you want to be careful to select neutral items that fit the type of house you are selling.

When you are doing your TV research, especially watch shows which focus on selling or renting property (as opposed to the home makeover shows catering to the homeowner).

Go to open houses

One of my favorite strategies for understanding my market is to attend open houses. In my area, they are on Sunday between 12 and 4 pm.

I target a certain price range within my market. For example, if I am renovating a house I want to sell for $150,000, I target houses in the same town that are selling between $125 and $175k.

As I walk through the houses, I am going through my checklist to see what my competition is doing, noting:

→ The overall condition
→ What has been renovated? Windows, roof, mechanicals?

➔ What level of materials are they using? e.g., are the countertops made out of granite or laminate, are the floors hard wood, tile, or laminate?

➔ The exterior appearance, landscaping, window shutters garage doors.

Then I take my notes and compare them to my current project While I am at the open house, I introduce myself to the hosting real estate agent and tell her the types of properties I am looking to buy.

The biggest mistake rehabbers make is that they often over rehab the house. They spend money when they don't need to. You only need to renovate to the level in your market. For example, if you install granite when the other houses in the neighborhood use a less expensive material, maybe you have spent money you didn't need to spend. Wouldn't you rather have those dollars in your pocket?

Maybe you renovate 10% better to sell the property faster or to demand a slightly higher price. Note that sometimes you can include an accent or a special feature to help your house sell faster. Continuing the previous example, you might decide to install a granite countertop because you have studied your competition and feel that the granite will sell your house faster Sometimes, rehabbers have added a special shower feature or a double sink in the master bathroom.

WARNING: Remember you are walking through houses that are for sale – they haven't sold yet. There is no guarantee the homeowners will get the price they want. You may want to track the houses and find out their actual sales price so that you truly understand what sells and at what price.

Study houses online

With the current technology, you can study your competition from the comfort of your own home. However, the photos will give you a good idea of the materials you should use as well as the condition your property should be in so that you can sell it or rent it at your target price. If done properly, these listings are almost as good as walking through a property.

Of course, the photos usually do not show you the flaws or lived-in features of the house. However, they will give you a good idea of materials and condition that properties are in to sell for that price.

Using your insight as a woman and the skills of a rehabber, you are now well on your way to rehabbing houses and apartments that will sell or rent quickly.

G and P were buying a condominium to rehab. The wonderful feature of condos is that they are all alike within one complex so it is simpler to determine their value. G and P were able to retrieve listings and photos of properties that had already sold. They were able to see what materials were used and what design changes were made without physically walking through the units. They were then able to make educated choices for rehabbing their unit and to predict the price they would be able to sell it for.

Family budgets, clipping coupons & scopes of work

Women know how to budget

With the life skills that we have, women are well-suited to this part of real estate.

We have already discussed how women, on the whole, make less than men. We have already said that many women face the situation of raising their children on one salary.

So haven't you become really good at making ends meet?

The grocery list

As far back as I can remember, my mom would write out a grocery list. It was like a scavenger hunt. My sisters and I would go up and down the aisles searching for the items on the list. If we saw something we wanted that was not on the list, Mom would often say "no". After all, she had a budget for groceries and she had to stick to it.

Then when I was a Junior Girl Scout in elementary school I earned the Cook's Badge. As part of this badge, my patrol planned a meal. We had to look at the cookbook, read the recipes, and make a list of the ingredients needed to make the meal. Then we looked in the newspaper to see if there were any coupons for those items. We were given a set amount of money and we had to find all the ingredients and stay within our budget.

Does this sound familiar to you?

Budgeting

When my good friend was growing up, she watched her maiden aunts manage money. Every week when they got paid they divided up the money into different envelopes. Perhaps the envelopes were for rent, electricity, phone, heat, food, and clothing. This was a physical reminder of the amount of money they had available to cover all of their needs.

Now my friend's daughter does the same thing. Only she uses online banking to divide up the family income into different accounts. When the money for groceries runs out, she has to wait until the next pay day. At first, this was difficult for her to do. She was used to spending money without thinking about it. However, she now really appreciates the discipline associated with budgeting. She and her husband live in a very nice home in a nice neighborhood and she is able to stay home and home school their children. She has choices that many of her friends don't.

Couponing

Have you ever watched one of those extreme couponing shows? Have you been amazed to see the amount of groceries the contestants can buy for less than $20?

Now these women are called "extreme couponers" for a

reason. However, there is a lesson for all of us to learn.

It is possible to buy ten items and get paid to do it. If you have the right coupons, and if the store doubles or triples the value of coupons, you're actually getting paid to go shopping!

I understand you probably don't need ten tubes of toothpaste (or whatever the special that week is). And I think that some of these couponers have become hoarders because they are so caught up in the game of saving money.

However, doesn't this open up the possibility that you can buy anything and get paid to do so?

Suggestion: Use coupons for a week. Clip all the coupons you can get and go shopping. See how well you can play this game. If you end up having more products than you need, feel free to distribute to your neighbors or give to a homeless shelter or veteran's organization. After all, you probably didn't pay anything for the items you are giving away!

HINT 1: Sign up for the email list for your favorite stores. (You can always set up a free email just for this purpose so your regular email account does not fill up with spam.) You will receive amazing members-only discounts. Just file them in a coupon folder so you can easily search for them when you need them. Recently, I popped into a clothing store to buy a pair of sneakers. Fortunately I remembered to search my email for a coupon and I saved 25%!

HINT 2: Before you buy anything, search online for a coupon. Simply enter the word coupon followed by the store or the item. I recently saved 80% on website domain names I was purchasing, simply because I took a moment to do that search.

Stretching a dollar

Again when growing up, I remember having breakfast for dinner. As kids, we thought it was cool to cut a circle in a slice of bread and cook an egg inside it. It was out of the ordinary so we had fun with it. For all I know, Mom was either trying to stretch the budget or clean out the refrigerator before buying groceries.

At camp, we used to make Hobo or Campfire stew. All we did was throw ground beef, cans of soup and whatever vegetables lying around into a big pot. It was cheap but filling. And we used up all the resources we had around us.

Bargain shopping: yes, you can negotiate for less

Nowadays most of us buy everything from big box stores. You walk into the store and the price tag is on it. We take the item to the cashier and pay for it.

Did you know you can actually ask for a discount on that item?

We bought tile for the bathroom in one of our properties. The contractor saw there were broken tiles so he took them back to the store. The employee not only helped him find the tile he needed, she also gave us a box of tile for free to compensate us for our trouble.

Look for product closeouts. Each store has a way of marking items they are discounting and/or discontinuing. If you are fortunate enough to figure out the system, you can pick up building supplies for as little as a penny each! The crazy thing is that they often just throw inventory in the trash.

Ask for a "good gal" discount. I heard this one on television during one holiday season. Walk up to the counter with a big smile on your face. Build a rapport

> with the employee. Then say something like, "You seem like a nice person. I know I am a nice person. Do you have a "good gal" discount by any chance? Amazingly this has worked for me multiple times while renting a car, buying jewelry or printing brochures. Coupons, discounts, and secret pre-sale bargains just seem to appear.

So yes, as women, we have many life experiences which help us in setting up a scope of work (grocery list), and bargain hunting (coupons), and negotiating (think farmer's market).

Setting up a scope of work

In the last chapter, we discussed how you want to keep the end in mind when you are renovating a property. Your end goal, your exit strategy, is going to determine what you are going to renovate and what you are going to leave as is.

So the first thing you will want to do is to define the scope of work. Your scope of work is simply a list – a specific list of renovation tasks.

General list

First start with generalities, a broad stroke. As you walk through the property, use this checklist and make a list of the items that need to be removed, improved, or totally renovated:

- Roof
- Windows
- Floors
- Kitchen
- Bathroom
- Heating and cooling
- Structural changes
- Electrical improvements
- Plumbing

Get more specific

The next step is to walk through the property with someone who has strong contracting experience. That may be you, of course.

> ➤ You may want to use a general contractor. This is someone that has experience in all things real estate.

> ➤ You may need to bring in several contractors to help you identify issues and estimate repairs. For example, you may want to bring in an electrician, a roofer, and an HVAC (heating, ventilation, and air conditioning) contractor.

> ➤ You may want to involve a licensed home inspector. I recommend you hire someone who has been a contractor for at least ten years.

In all cases, walk through the property with the professional. You want to make sure they do a thorough job for you. Plus you will get on-the-job training.

You will need to pay the home inspector to get their report. Often the contractors will not charge you because they are hoping to get the job when you buy the property. So you will only want to engage these people when you are serious about purchasing the property.

Don't depend on your memory

When you walk through the property, the contractors are tempted to give you an estimate as a "guesstimate". And you may be tempted to just use this figure. The only problem with this idea is that you can lose thousands of dollars because you will miss or forget something.

So grab your camera, measuring tape, tape recorder, and paper/pencil. The more specific your measurements, the more accurate will be your estimate. Also, you will be able to refer to your photos, measurements and notes in the future as your project progresses.

Get even more specific

Your final scope of work is going to include the materials you are going to use. For example:

- ➤ Number and size of doors: bedroom, closet, garage, and exit doors
- ➤ Number of switch plates
- ➤ Color of paint
- ➤ SKU (stock keeping unit) and/or model number for bathroom vanities, faucets, light fixtures and more

You will also make a list of specific tasks to be done. I organize this by room and also by specialty. For example, I might have an electrical scope of work, plumbing scope of work, and flooring scope of work.

Creating your budget

With your specific scope of work, you can start getting estimates from your contractor. With a specific scope of work, you can interview three to five contractors and be able to compare quotes.

Don't be afraid to negotiate on pricing and on the tasks that are included in the price. Refer back to the chapter on negotiating.

You will want to add in a contingency fund. Add in 10-15% of your budget to allow for unexpected repairs. For example, you may find that you need to take care of termite damage. One time, we discovered we had to totally replace the dryer ductwork and venting when we opened up the wall in the bathroom. If your budget is $50,000 for repairs, I recommend you budget another $10,000 for contingencies. If you don't need it, you will have more profit.

Creating your timeline

Once you have your scopes of work together, you will want to set up a schedule. Some tasks can be done at the same time. Some tasks need to be done in chronological order. Recently I had a plumber, electrician, framer, and HVAC installer working on the house all at the same time. It was like a ballet where everyone knew their tasks and worked with and around each other.

Your job is to motivate the contractors to get the job done within the time limit you have set. After all, it is your pocketbook that will suffer if the project takes longer than you expected.

Stick to your plan

It is so important for you to stick to the plan you created for this project. Just like you need to stay within your home budget and your grocery list, it is even more important for you to stay true to the scope of work you have created.

Of course, surprises do come up from time to time. However the more experienced you and your contractors are, the more specific your estimate of repairs, the fewer surprises you should have.

Warning: You will be tempted to buy a more expensive vanity or add in crown molding or select a fancy door. You need to discipline yourself not to do this. You will add days to the project and you will spend more money on labor and materials than you had intended.

When lemons appear, make lemonade

Along the way, you may discover some unpleasant surprises. This is when your creativity, your lack of drama, and your positive attitude plays a big part.

When your building inspector informs you something doesn't meet the code, your job is to figure out a solution that works for your project, your budget, and your inspector.

> My students, RB and LT, proved their mettle while rehabbing their first project. After a heavy downpour, the basement started filling up with water. This was a basement that they were finishing with carpet, dry wall, and tile. Not just a little bit of water – inches of water. They called their contractor who started giving them a huge price to fix the problem. As RT calmly studied the problem, he realized the downspout was draining into the ground right next to the basement. So he hand-dug some shallow trenches and purchased some drain tubing so that the water would drain far away from the house and spread onto the lawn. Problem solved for less than $100!

When one contractor tattles about another contractor, use your skills of settling squabbles between your children. Get the facts and make the best decision you can to sort it out.

Sometimes not being a contractor has given me an advantage. Because I don't know the answer, I ask a lot of questions. I separate the facts from the angst around the situation. And then I have been able to arrive at a solution that works.

I had one contractor who is a very good contractor. However, he also loved to be dramatic. He would say things like, "This is a problem. A very big problem." Most of the time he was able to create a simple solution so he would look like the hero.

My painter didn't work on Saturdays to honor the Sabbath. And I was up against my timeline because freezing cold weather was coming. We just HAD to finish the exterior paint that weekend. So my general contractor brought in two painters to work on Saturday (their Sabbath was on Sunday).

Saturday morning, my contractor called me in a panic. Linda, we have a big problem, a really big problem. The exterior siding shows two tones of paint! We have to paint the entire siding again and my guys were here to just do some touch-ups! I told him to call the paint store to find out what happened. However, he was so upset that he couldn't figure out a solution. I left my other location and drove thirty-five minutes to the job site. Sure enough, there were two tones of paint. It looked like my regular painter had bought paint that didn't match.

I took a deep breath. I looked for the cans of paint the guys were using but the numbers were covered with paint. My GC and I went to the paint store with the paint. The paint numbers looked right but the paint on the building didn't match. The paint store employee looked up our account (fortunately the painter had created a sub-account with my property name on it). And then the employee solved the mystery. My painter had purchased some paint at half-tone to act as a primer. So when the paint was wet, it looked different and when it was dry it matched! So crisis was resolved. Actually, there was no crisis. Just a breakdown in communication. If my GC had not reacted so strongly, we could have resolved the issue over the phone. It pays to stay cool, calm and collected.

Keep good records and balance your checkbook

Finally, just as you need to do for your family, keep good records and balance your checkbook. Your contractors want to be paid as soon as the job is done. Just make sure that the job is done before you pay them. If the work is tied to an inspection, hold back enough money to ensure the work will pass inspection.

It is a good idea to have a spreadsheet that shows the amount you budgeted for the job and the actual amount spent. This will help you estimate future jobs.

Keep track of all receipts. You want to get 100% credit on your tax returns. Plus it's always easier to return excess materials if you have the right receipts.

Acknowledge yourself for a job well done

How do you celebrate accomplishments in your family? Growing up, we hardly ever ate out. Eating pizza or fried chicken from a take-out restaurant was a big treat. Our family celebrated our accomplishments like learning how to ride a bike or swimming a lap of the pool or doing well in school with a take-out dinner. It was special!

Do the same thing for yourself. As you are building your business, you will want to re-invest your profits back into your company. Be sure to treat yourself, and your team, to something you can afford. You will remember this as a special occasion.

It is also a great idea to note what worked, and what didn't work, about the project. You will learn from this experience to make each future project better and more and more profitable.

You're in charge

No glass ceiling here

ALTHOUGH WOMEN ARE BREAKING through the glass ceiling every day in the United States, it's still a struggle. Women still earn only 81% of what men make for the same job. Among full time adult workers in the first quarter of 2016, women made $779 per week compared to men who made $963 (81% of men's earnings).[24]

Unfortunately, depending on your job category, you may be making only 69% of what your male counterpart is paid. If you think this only happens with unskilled labor, think again. Women represent 1 of 3 physicians and surgeons but they earn only 69 cents for every dollar their male colleagues earn. Male physicians made $202,533 on average in 2013, while female doctors had a median income of $140,036 that year."[25]

---

24 "Labour Force Statistics", Bureau of Labour Statistics, www.bls.gov/webapps/legacy/cpswktab2.htm (accessed July 16 2016).
25 Herman, Bob, "Male-female pay disparities abound in healthcare professions", *Modern Healthcare,* March 16 2015, www.modernhealthcare.com/article/20150316/NEWS/150319919 (accessed July 16 2016).

We may be starting to turn the tide on this issue. In December 2015 *Fortune Magazine* reported this exciting breakthrough:

As a rule, women make less than men in the U.S., making about 77 cents for every dollar a man makes. Yet when it comes to the salaries of corporate finance leaders, it's the men who have catching up to do.

> A new study by executive compensation firm Equilar and the Associated Press found that female CFOs at S&P 500 companies made more than their male counterparts in 2014, according to the Associated Press. On average, women finance chiefs made about $200,000 more than men, with a median salary of $3.32 million.
>
> Female CFOs' salaries are also growing faster than those of male CFOs; last year, women's earnings increased by 11%, while men's earnings increased by 7%, according to the report.[26]

The wonderful benefit about being a real estate entrepreneur (or any entrepreneur) is that you can be rewarded for your efforts regardless of who you are. This is true for women, minorities and men.

It doesn't matter whether you have a PhD, went to a certain school or have a certain upbringing. You don't have to belong to a yacht club. You don't have to be born on the right side of the tracks. You don't have to be a certain color or gender. An entrepreneur is truly an equal opportunity employer because you are the employer!

This opportunity has resulted in many women (and other minorities) becoming multi-millionaires through real estate. No one is limited.

What characteristics will contribute to your success? What is

---

26 Zarya, Valentina, "Women Make More than Men in This C-Level Position" Fortune.com, December 18 2015, fortune.com/2015/12/18/women-men-cfo (accessed July 16 2016).

especially unique about you? You don't have to beat your brains against the wall, trying to be someone you're not. You simply need to be you, get training to fill in the gaps, and take action.

Start with what you are already good at

I have mentored hundreds of students, many of whom are discovering real estate for the first time. Their faces have that confused look like they are learning a whole new language. What is this ARV, MAO, FMV, CMA, REO stuff?"[27] I will explain these terms in much more detail in *Women Are Simply Better At Getting Started in Real Estate.*

They forget that they either own a house, live in a house, or rent an apartment. They have probably played Monopoly or the Game of Life at some point.

You are not starting from scratch.

My favorite student in this regard is DR. He is a commercial pilot, a veteran, a family man and all around adventurer. He had this idea that he should invest in apartments to increase his cash flow and enhance his retirement, but knew nothing about real estate. In a property management course, I gave the assignment to create a rental ad to attract good paying tenants. If they didn't own any apartments, I suggested they look online and create an ad for someone else's building. Most students didn't do anything.

What did DR do? He created a whole slide show for renting the Taj Mahal!

In less than a year and a half, DR and his business partner had acquired 19 units with very strong cash flow!

27 After repair value; maximum allowable offer; fair market value; comparable market analysis and real estate owned. REO means that the bank has already foreclosed on the property and now has the deed.

What are your skills?

If you are reading this book, you are already successful. You have a lifetime of experience. Your talent and experience will help you succeed in real estate.

- → Multi-tasking
- → Disciplining children
- → Creative (arts, music, thinking outside the box)
- → Marketing (have you ever run for class president or managed a bake sale?)
- → Creating posts for social media, websites, photography
- → Raising capital
- → Writing term papers or business plans
- → Playing on a team, performing in a band or participating in a school musical

You get the idea.

Take a few minutes and make a list of every little thing you have a talent for or have experience in (including adopting animals, earning Scout badges, cooking, painting your room as a kid, decorating your own home, or fixing a leaky faucet). Then think about how that can apply to you investing in real estate.

Skill/experience	How this applies to real estate

Here are some examples of how you might complete this chart:

Skill/experience	How this applies to real estate
Balance the family checkbook, buy groceries and clothes, pay doctors	Manage the rehab budget for both materials and labor
Your friends love the way you decorate your house	Stage your property for sale or rent
You get lots of "likes" on your social media posts	Use your social media skills to advertise open houses, find contractors, and buy more deals

As you read this book, you will begin to see how you can build on your life experience to create success in real estate.

You are in charge

Imagine being CEO of your own company. You have broken the glass ceiling. You have the right to hire and to fire. You can give out promotions and demotions. You make the choices. You write the checks. You are the one creating jobs instead of the one hoping to have a job and hoping to get paid. You are creating your own economy. You don't have to read the news, because you're busy making news.

Consider this: each piece of real estate is a business

> Business:
> The activity of making, buying, or selling goods or providing services in exchange for money
> *Merriam-Webster Dictionary*

I was sitting in a seminar where we were discussing how to set up your business to be sold. As I was listening I had a shocking revelation. Each of my multi-family houses was actually a business!

Instead of real estate investing being a get rich quick scheme it's really a form of business. Every time you acquire a new piece of real estate, you are acquiring a new business. With each property, you should have a business plan which includes:

➤ An acquisition plan
- o How you are going to finance it
- o Who is going to own it, for example, by yourself with partners, in an LLC, a trust?

➤ A management plan
- o What you are going to renovate
- o A breakdown of costs
- o A budget for capital improvements
- o Methods for screening and managing tenants

➤ An exit strategy (preferably two)
- o Are you going to rent it long term?
- o Or rent it to someone who will later buy it?
- o Or sell it as quickly as possible?

If you have another business, this thought process also applies.

112

Women are extraordinarily successful at building real estate portfolios

You really are the CEO of your own company. You are in charge. For many women, this experience is so liberating that they buy one property, then another, then another ... well, you get the picture.

I have met so many women who have literally built million-dollar real estate empires and their husbands don't know anything about it. Many of these women came of age before the women's liberation movement.

> Victoria Kaplan is the oldest real estate broker in Connecticut. She bought her first 2-family house at age 18 and her office building at 25. Fifty years later, her companies own a portfolio of hundreds of single and multi-family properties.

> Pearl Lagasse came from a family of brothers in the real estate rental market. In fact, her brother Paul was one of my mentors. Not to be outdone, she started acquiring properties on her own. In her seventies when I interviewed her, she was very proud of the fact that she hired handymen to do the work and provided housing for many people.

Sue Nelson now owns over 1,500 units across America while her husband continues to teach music in the local school. She provides jobs for over forty people. When I toured some of her properties, I was struck by how many people thanked her for creating their job so they could buy their own home. Why did she get started? Her daughter was born with special needs. Sue needed to find a way to stay home and pay for all the medical care so that her daughter could have a better quality of life.

Robyn Thompson has rehabbed over 300 properties. She even finished fifty-one in a single year! Why did she get started? She was about to be laid off from IBM and needed a way to pay her mortgage. Now she has the time and money to breed horses on her beautiful ranch in Florida.

Joya Johnson is a third generation female African-American real estate investor. Her grandmother bought a rooming house in Washington DC. However, in those days, a woman could not buy property or borrow money so she bought it with owner financing. She then handed it down to Joya's mother and Joya still runs the property. Building on her grandmother's legacy, Joya is a very successful real estate broker, rehabber and developer.

Name your title: CEO, President, Division Manager

Have you heard of sales trainer Brian Tracy? He taught me how to sell and has trained entrepreneurs for generations. When I attended one of his workshops, he said something revolutionary: This is your own company. You can give yourself any title you choose."

Wow! You can call yourself CEO, President, Property Manager or anything you want. One of my students calls himself "Eastern District Acquisition Manager". By the way, there is no other district manager! I once called myself *Chief Empowerment Officer.*

Titles are important. Your title conveys an image to the person who receives your business card. You can have multiple business cards with multiple titles. One for marketing, one for meeting professionals, one for your tenants and so on.

Go ahead. Give yourself a title and know you have broken the glass ceiling. You are a real estate entrepreneur.

NOTE: When you create a business card for your tenants, I recommend your title be Property Manager or Handywoman. You do not want your tenants to know that you are the owner of the building. When your tenants ask you if they can get a break on their rent, for example, you can say that you would love to help them out but that you are not the owner and cannot make that decision.

What skills do you need to be a strong business owner?

There are many skills that will contribute to your success as a business owner. Your life skills have already prepared you for this moment.

Firstly you need to take charge of the situation. Be clear with each person that you are the decision maker – the buck stops with you. You lay out the funding and therefore you make the decisions.

Secondly, you raise the funding. This means you will be completing mortgage applications and building relationships with people who can lend you funds without going to a bank. You will be creating a credibility package to explain why you are a credible borrower and why your project is worth the investment for the lender. Refer to *Women Are Simply Better at Finding Money to Buy Real Estate.*

Thirdly, you will be negotiating the purchase and the sale of the property. This takes finesse.

And fourthly, you will be responsible for hiring contractors, rehabbing properties, negotiating contracts, and negotiating material prices. "But wait, Linda", you say, "I don't even know what a hammer looks like". If that is the case, you will learn construction with experience. In the meantime, you can look for someone you trust who can help you think through these decisions.

I recently renovated a single family house. Before I purchased it, I had a choice of three contractors I planned to use to be the general contractor. For various reasons, none of these worked out.

As CEO, I needed to quickly find the right person for the job. I asked for referrals, and went on Craigslist. I interviewed about six contractors. Finally, I found one I wanted to work with. Besides his knowledge and experience and pricing, I hired him because I knew he would communicate with me. He treated me with respect, included me on all decisions, and patiently explained what I did not understand.

Fifth, you will be responsible for screening and managing tenants – and you will need to know the laws in your state for screening tenants and for removing tenants. Evicting tenants and midnight calls about toilets are the two biggest fears preventing women from becoming property owners. However, when you know how to screen tenants, and when you stop accepting excuses for non-payment, you will eliminate or greatly reduce the need to evict tenants. Also, proper regular maintenance of your properties will virtually eliminate those midnight emergencies.

Sixth, you will be responsible for your business accounts. A beautiful thing about being an entrepreneur is that you suddenly have tax write-offs you didn't have as a regular employee. Even better, as a property owner, you can depreciate your building and save money on taxes while making money with positive cash flow. It is important for you to be educated about these tax write-offs and to maintain proper bookkeeping to take full advantage of them. I'm not saying you are going to suddenly become a CPA. Instead, you want to become aware of the tax laws affecting real estate so you can ask questions. You want to hire a CPA who is very familiar with real estate transactions and rental properties.

Finally, you will be the person accountable for selling your property. For short-term flips, this means you want to stage the property to get the highest price. You also want to determine your selling strategy. Do you want to sell it yourself? Do you want to auction it off? Do you want to hire a real estate agent? The decisions you make here can either lose or gain you thousands of dollars.

That's it! These are your accountabilities. You are now in control of your destiny.

You have broken through the glass ceiling!

Your mindset creates your bank account

YOUR JOB AS A REAL ESTATE ENTREPENEUR is to make money. I know that sounds obvious but sometimes we get enthralled with the deal. "I love the house", "This is such a cute neighborhood", "Did you see the built-ins?". We get so excited that we forget to do our due diligence to make sure we are going to make money.

We are just so excited that someone has called on our marketing and she wants to sell us her house that we try to make it into a deal when it isn't one.

So many times, a student will bring me a lead. I review the information she sends me about the project and give her advice so she can make an offer. But then she obsesses over it for weeks. She will spend two weeks analyzing the value of the property. She brings in three contractors to figure out the cost of repairs and then she tries to figure out where the money is coming from.

Finally! She is ready to make an offer! Excitedly, she waits to hear the good news. Unfortunately, by that time, the property is already under contract to someone else!

One of my teachers told me, "You can't steal in slow motion. If you think it's a deal, you need to move fast! You need to do your due diligence quickly, negotiate quickly, and make your offer before anyone else knows about the property. Of course with training, practice, and experience, you will get more accurate and faster. However, the biggest time waster is between your ears.

For right now, I want you to notice how much your mindset can impact your success. Don't worry. In the upcoming books in this series, we will show you how to do your due diligence how to negotiate terms, and how to cover your tracks so you make profitable offers. Right now let's focus on mindset.

Your mindset creates your bank account

Why didn't my student make an offer immediately after we discussed it? Her mindset, her fear, her paralysis from analysis kept her from making offers.

I have seen people who have perfect credit, have lots of money in the bank, and have construction experience who never make a deal! On the other hand, I have other students who barely know anything and barely have two coins to rub together. Yet, they make an offer in less than sixty days!

What is the difference?

Mindset!

If you are anything like me, you are about to skip this chapter and get to the good stuff, the nitty-gritty-here-is-my-to-do-list stuff.

WARNING! This may be the *most* important chapter of this book. As I just said, I have seen some of the most qualified people in the world come through my coaching and never buy a property. And then I have seen students without money or credit and they bought a property faster than anyone else.

What is mindset, anyway?

> Mindset:
> A fixed mental attitude or disposition that predetermines a person's responses to and interpretations of situations.
> An inclination or a habit.
>
> *Merriam-Webster Dictionary*

In real life, what does this mean? Let me share an example from two different students.

I just received an email from someone who was angry and disappointed because she thought our classes would meet every other week and the classes met every week instead. Because of her busy schedule, she couldn't attend all of them. Therefore, in her mind, she doesn't know enough and can't make any offers on any properties. (Keep in mind that all of the class material is online and accessible twenty-four hours a day, plus she can email me about any real estate deal and I will analyze it for her since she is one of my students.)

Now compare this to a student who started our program in the summer, months before the live classes started. In six months, she had purchased six units with 96% owner financing. She just started swinging the bat way before she had all the training.

Student A had a mindset of blaming others.

Student B had a mindset of being successful no matter what.

Student A never called her coach.

Student B called her coaches (yes all of us) multiple times a week.

Student A found a partner who was also too busy to attend class or too busy to do anything even though he has a construction career.

Student B left a high paying career to take care of her two

young children and had to make money in this business or else. When she told her husband the deal had closed, he was surprised she had purchased three buildings (not just one). In other words, Student B has been doing this on her own, without input from her husband.

Which student are you? A or B?

The problem is ...

Here is another example of mindset. Have you ever heard someone (including yourself) say:

> *The problem is ...*
> *I can't because ...*
> *You can't do that because ...*
> *That's impossible ....*
> *It's hard because ....*
> *I don't want to give you excuses but ...*
> *I tried but ...*

If you listen to everyday conversations, you will hear statements like these. Unfortunately, you will hear people say the same phrase over and over again. And then they back it up with giving you a logical explanation. (At least the explanation is logical to them.)

➢ *I don't have time.*
  o You and I have the same 24 hours a day, 7 days a week, 365 days a year.
➢ *I don't have enough money.*
➢ *I don't know enough.*
➢ *My _____ says you can't do this.*
  o Real estate agent: It's not their fault. Real estate school teaches practices and principles. It doesn't teach you how to do marketing, negotiate contracts or structure creative financing.

122

o   Attorney: Many attorneys are not real estate attorneys. Even within the real estate discipline, many attorneys are not familiar with wholesaling, owner financing and other creative deal structuring. You must find an attorney who is familiar with these concepts. You will explain what you are attempting to accomplish. Then her job is to set up the legal wording of the contract.

o   Contractor: No offense to contractors, but contractors know what they know – they do not know everything. For example, many contractors have not built from a blueprint, they do not know all of the building codes, they do not know how to manage a rehab budget, they do not know how to manage their crew/subcontractors, and they often don't know how to solve a problem in a 100+ year old house.

o   Contractor Part 2: Contractors usually get paid by homeowners to do a project. The homeowner does not need to make a profit – she is only trying to improve her home. As rehabbers, we must make a profit. Contractors do not have the mindset of a rehabber. As the rehabber, we have to make the decisions about what to rehab/what not to rehab, and what materials to use/what not to use.

o   Friend and co-workers. Stop listening to broke people! Stop listening to people with an employee mentality! They kill your possibility before you even get started. They have their own mindset issues to deal with.

o   Uncle, Mom, Dad, sibling: They remember you being the ten-year-old screw-up and forget that you are an intelligent, creative-thinking, adult now.

Who is *your* naysayer?  _____

> When I first started buying real estate, I was still an insurance agent. I was an active member of a weekly networking group. The real estate agent in the group told me "You will never be able to do this. If it is a good deal, the agents will buy up the deal first." Imagine if I had listened to him. I would not have the life I have today.

Complaining or negative possibility

Have you ever stood in line at a coffee shop or grocery store? Of course you have. Ever listen to what people say to each other?

The weather looks bad today, doesn't it?
I can't wait until the weekend.
Why is this line so slow?

You get the picture. In my experience, people in line tend to talk about negative things. I think it is because human beings tend to bond with each other over negativity.

When I was a technical writer subcontractor for DuPont, my team would eat together in the cafeteria almost every day. What would the conversation be about?

→ The weather
→ Sports
→ Gossip about others
→ What we were going to do on the weekend or what we just did on the weekend

I got bored really quickly with this. I took it upon myself to have a new topic of conversation for each lunch. All of a sudden we started having lively discussions about all kinds of subjects.

Over time, I noticed that we built stronger working relationships by seeing each other as people (not just co-workers). By hearing other people's points of view, my mind really opened up on all sorts of topics. I also noticed we would return to work happier and feeling more refreshed.

This is a simple mindset shift exercise anyone can do. How will you implement this idea?

Next time you're standing in line, try this

Next time you find yourself standing in line, or in an elevator, or at a party, try these lines to get the conversation going in the right direction:

What's good about today?
What do you want to brag about?
What are you looking forward to?

People will give you a startled look for sure. Just smile and ask again. Sometimes when I am in the grocery store and I see someone holding a vegetable I am not familiar with, I will ask them, "How do you cook that?" or "What's your favorite recipe for that?" You will make a new friend over exotic foods.

When I am lost, I will ask for directions. People love to help and they feel better about themselves. Give them that opportunity.

As you pass people on the street say, "Good morning" or "Hi, how are you doing today?"

I even talk to the cashier or the waitress. Even the cranky ones! Remember that these women are on their feet eight hours a day dealing with customers. They are probably getting little more than minimum wage and may have troubles at home. Say hello and ask them how their day is going.

If they are cranky, say something like, "Are you having a tough day?" You will be amazed. They will smile and thank you for caring. As a bonus, you will get much better service.

What does this have to do with real estate or business?

Why am I having you do this? Real estate is a contact sport. You make the best deals when you can talk directly to the owner and when the owner likes you. You also find the best off-market deals with word-of-mouth marketing. This exercise gives you practice.

Once you start these friendly conversations, you can share what you are doing and ask for referrals, you can ask for a better deal on a rental car, and you can request an increase in your credit limit.

Of course, you are also making your world a happier place. Isn't that a good enough reason?

Myths about personal development

There are a lot of common myths about personal development. One is that it's only for people who have something wrong with them or who can't be successful on their own. Or it takes too much time, it's hard work and it's expensive. A lot of times I hear this is the namby-pamby, airy-fairy stuff. So many times I hear: "I'll worry about that personal development, I'll worry about health and relationships and family – *after* I hit my goals and financial success."

Well, the truth is that personal development is the **key** to your success. In fact, I would venture to say that personal development is not just a nice idea, it is **critical** to your success. Why do I say this? Well, have you read *Think and Grow Rich* by Napoleon Hill? How about *Rich Dad Poor Dad* by Robert Kiyosaki? Or anything by sales trainer and business consultant Brian Tracey? Or *Secrets of the Millionaire Mind* by T. Harv Eker? How about Arianna Huffington's book *Thrive*? Each of these books are actually personal development books as well as powerful business books.

126

Why live your best life?

I believe that you can live your life the way you design it. And the opportunity is now. Despite what the media and the news would have us believe, we live in a time where truly anything is possible. In this book, we focus on your ability to have your own business and of profiting from real estate. But we could just as easily discuss possibilities in any area of your life: health, relationships, family. If it's possible for you to live your best life, why live one more moment in pain, stress, or poverty?

You deserve this

You deserve this, and if your mind does not believe you, listen to me. As an independent observer of your life, I say that you deserve to live the life you want to live.

When I am talking to people in the real estate investing world, the entrepreneurship world, these are the challenges I see most people are facing. Are you facing any of them?

> ⇢ Are you laid off or afraid of being laid off? Actually, I talked to a woman last week who was thrilled she was laid off because she was excited about the opportunity ahead of her but most people will face that reality with dread.
> ⇢ Are you working one, two or more jobs that you don't like just to make ends meet?
> ⇢ Are you putting up with relationships that are negative and that pull you down? Are you maintaining relationships that do not support you in your business goals? I am talking about your spouse, your family, your co-workers, and even (especially) your friends.
> ⇢ What about your health? Perhaps you don't feel well, you are overweight or you are in pain.
> ⇢ And what about stress? Are you having fun? Living a balanced life?

A couple of years ago, I was in the middle of being incredibly busy with business and volunteer work and all of a sudden my body said: "Enough!"

A crippling illness hit me out of nowhere. One day I was fine exercising in the gym, and running a real estate seminar. The next morning, I was in so much pain with my back I couldn't walk. I literally had to tell my body to walk across the kitchen because it wouldn't move on its own.

All of a sudden, I had to deal with disability. It took me about a year to recover and I still have residual issues. If I hadn't had my rental income and my own business, I would have been in big trouble financially. I certainly couldn't work forty hours a week – I would have lost my job.

The doctors did all kinds of tests to diagnose me. What I had contracted usually indicated a serious long term disease. The tests came back: my attack was idiopathic (unknown). The doctor was ecstatic because she usually has to deliver bad news. However, for me, this was a mystery. How did this happen? What caused this?

With no medical reason to blame, I looked inside at my life. What, holistically, caused this to happen?

I had just taken on another huge responsibility as a volunteer. This was on top of everything else I was doing. My back, my spine, said "enough". Literally this was the straw that broke the camel's (my) back.

I got the message loud and clear. It was time for me to live a more balanced life. I slept at least ten hours a day (instead of four to six hours). I explored every medical and non-medical strategy to reduce or eliminate pain. These treatments were time-consuming – I lost ten to twenty hours a week in business productivity. In other words, my health became my business.

I resigned from my volunteer position. I started downsizing our real estate assets by eliminating properties in challenging areas. I started delegating more. I gave myself permission to focus on what I wanted to focus on and not always say yes to others.

When something like this happens to you, everyone wants to know what happened. In this moment, you have two choices.

Tell the story from beginning to end, reliving the gory details.

You will get lots of sympathy from people. Some of this sympathy is a disguise for people who want to see you weak. Some of this sympathy is in the form of reality TV where people enjoy hearing about tragedy. Obviously, many people in your life want to sympathize with you to help you feel better. Unfortunately, this strategy reinforces your experience over and over again, making the pain more real and keeping you stuck.

or-

Do what I did. I simply started declaring:

Every day is a better day.

And you know what? Every day did become a better day. In the beginning, I felt like I was faking it to make it. I was saying that "every day is a better day" without any evidence. I was simply declaring this new reality. And then, I started seeing a little bit of progress every day. And then every once in a while, I would have a huge breakthrough. I would stop tripping over my feet or I would stop falling down when I ran. I would experience days of being pain-free.

Declaring "every day is a better day" created the mindset for me to be open to any suggestion for healing. Shonda Rhimes recently wrote a book called *The Year of Yes*. This was my year of yes. If someone had a suggestion for alleviating pain, I was all over it. And believe me, when you have an illness, everyone and their aunt has a suggestion for healing. Some of them were pretty crazy. But the ones that worked, led to other strategies that worked. And *every day is a better day* became reality.

Produce a breakthrough

I AM SHARING THIS BREAKTHROUGH TECHNOLOGY with you so that you can see the power of mindset and be open to possibilities around you. Now it's your turn to create a breakthrough! I am going to show you how to achieve a breakthrough in seven easy steps.

So who is this breakthrough technology good for?

You, if:

→ You are at the top of your game and you are looking for that extra edge.

→ You are not satisfied and you are ready and open for new possibilities.

→ You hear yourself complain about the same thing (or same someone) over and over again.

→ You are not producing the results you expected even after investing in training and taking action.

→ And really anyone ten years old to one hundred, entrepreneur or employee, male or female, rich or poor.

Let's go over the seven steps of what it takes to cause a breakthrough in your life. I am going to walk you through each step in great detail. If you have not done so already, grab a paper and pencil so we can work together. You may want to make a copy of the chart at the end of this chapter.

Step 1

Step 1 is to select one area to focus on. It really doesn't matter which one area you focus on because success in one area of life will carry over to other areas. And of course, you can repeat this process over and over again for each area of your life.

Go ahead, select one area you want to focus on right now for this exercise. For example, select an issue in the area of health, relationships, career, business success or happiness. See if you can have a specific area. For example, you may want to focus on weight management, your children, or your ability to make money in real estate. You may want to focus on calling motivated sellers or on raising private funds.

Step 2

Step 2 is to discover where you are right now. After all, you can't get anywhere unless you know where you are right now. So close your eyes for a moment. It's okay. Nobody is looking at you and nobody is going to laugh at you. Just close your eyes right now and scan that area of life for yourself right now.

> ➤ What is it like right now, that area of life that you selected?
> ➤ What's the struggle, what's the challenge?
> ➤ Where are you successful and where are you not successful?
> ➤ Are you feeling pain?
> ➤ Are you having any emotions about it?
> ➤ What are your thoughts or reasons around this issue?

Now I want you to open your eyes and I want you to write down the status quo. Write it down exactly. For example:

→ I weigh so much weight, I want to lose so much weight.
→ I feel like I am working 24 hours a day. How can I have time off?
→ I don't know what to say when a real estate seller calls me.

Write it down for yourself. What is your status quo?

Step 3

All right, now you know where you are, let's invent where you want to go.

Write down your goals. Just select one goal that we can work on right now as you read through this chapter. You can't get from here to there unless you know where you want to go. So, take a moment now and write that down for yourself. And by the way, you can take some notes now and then go back and do this exercise at another time, but I really would like for you to see a breakthrough as you are reading this chapter.

I invite you also to write down your dream day, your dream life, your dream job.

How powerful is this exercise? Have you ever watched the Olympics? Have you seen the athlete (especially a gymnast, a diver or a skier) as she closes her eyes and moves her head and arms as she envisions the event she is about to run? She creates a movie of her event, frame by frame. That's the idea.

Dr. Denis Waitley, Ph.D, states in The *Psychology of Winning*:

I took the visualization process from the Apollo program and instituted it during the 1980s and '90s" into the Olympic program. And it was called Visual Motor Rehearsal: 'When you visualize, then you materialize.' And the interesting thing about the mind is, we took Olympic athletes and then hooked them up to sophisticated biofeedback equipment and had them run their event ONLY in their mind. Incredibly, the same muscles fired, in the same sequence when they were running the race in their mind, as when they were running it on the track. How could this be? Because the mind can't distinguish whether you're really doing it or whether it's just a practice. If you've been there in your mind, you'll go there in the body.[28]

If you're going to invent your perfect day, your perfect real estate business, your perfect health, whatever area of life you are focusing on, I want you to imagine exactly what would that look like.

For example, your perfect real estate business day might look like this:

→ You check your bank account to see how much money your tenants have deposited.

→ Your assistant checks your email and phone messages and writes down all the messages from motivated sellers, qualified tenants, and rehabbers looking to buy from you.

→ You call the best leads and set up appointments for the week.

→ You attend a meeting with a seller to make an offer that will generate $55,600 after you rehab and sell it.

→ You celebrate by attending your kid's soccer game and treating the team to pizza.

OK, now it's your turn. So go ahead, close your eyes and envision your dream. You got it? Okay, good. Now I want you to open your eyes and write this down in living color. Go ahead. Write it down in living color.

Please note that you may find this difficult to do because of past failures. Many of my students come to me after dealing

---

28 Waitley, Denis E., *The Psychology of Winning,* Warner Books, 1992.

with foreclosure, bankruptcy, short sale, divorce, job loss, or other challenges. I feel your pain having gone through many challenges myself. However, you have a choice. You can focus on the pain from the past OR you can invent your future by focusing on your future with this exercise. How do you want to spend the next ten, thirty or even fifty years of your life? I can tell you that my successful students were the women who learned from the pain, focused on the future, and took action each and every day.

Step 4

During Step 4, I want you to discover what's holding you back. Is it a fear of failure, or of success? Is it a thought about yourself? What is holding you back?

Now discovering this may be a little bit difficult, a little bit hidden from you, because sometimes you have a blind spot. For example, imagine driving down the highway and you put on your right turn signal and start to move into the right lane. All of a sudden, you hear someone sitting on their horn. It turns out that she was driving a red motorcycle right beside you. You couldn't see her because she was driving in your blind spot and your mirrors didn't pick her up.

It's the same thing in life. We have these blind spots, these things that trip us up, because we are not aware of them. During Step Four, you are going to start noticing a thought or feeling or experience that trips you up when you are focused on your goal. For example, when you start cleaning your house, you see all this dust behind the sofa that you didn't know was there. You have to clean up all of the dust and all of a sudden you have a clean living space.

Here are some hints to help you identify what's holding you back or getting in the way of achieving your goal. See if you catch yourself saying any of these things over and over again:

The problem is ...

I can't because …
You can't do that because …
That's impossible …
It's hard because …
I don't want to give you excuses but …
I tried but …
I don't know how to …
I don't have time to …

Whatever you say in "…" is probably the thing that is holding you back. Try it out:

For example, let's say you want to call Owner Sarah Jones because you know if you buy her house, you will be able to make $25,000 after rehabbing the property. You realize you have been procrastinating calling on Owner Jones because she has been on your to do list for a week. What do you say to yourself each day as you re-write this task on your list?

➤ Monday: "I didn't have time today." So now you put this down as an appointment on your schedule. By the way, this is a great strategy. When you have a specific time, your mind tends to pay more attention than if this item is on a list of tasks.

➤ Tuesday: "I had an emergency with my child." The emergency is resolved and you rewrite this task for tomorrow. Note: You may want to ask yourself if this was really an emergency or could it have been handled in a different way.

➤ Wednesday: "I can't because I have to practice my script."

➤ Thursday/Friday: Another two days go by as you found excuses for not practicing the script. Hopefully you found a friend who will pretend to be Owner Jones so you can practice your script. Another way to practice is to stand in front of the mirror as you practice your script.

➤ And then the truth, the real reason, comes out. You get to the bottom line which may be "I am scared I will say something to screw up this deal" or "I am scared she will say 'yes' and I don't know what to do next!"

If you say the same thing over and over again, this is probably your stumbling block.

If you still have not identified a limiting belief, ask your spouse or your closest friends. Or talk to your coach or mentor or accountability partner. They know. It is easier for someone outside of you to identify the stop.

So I want you to write down whatever you came up with in this exercise.

Step 5

It's time for you to take action. You have figured out where you are, where you want to go, and what's holding you back. Now let's acknowledge that something is holding you back and take action any way. So let's set up your action plan and implement it.

Now here is the cool thing about this step:

➤ If you take action, you are going to produce a result.
   o If you don't produce the result you want, you can analyze what happened and put in the correction.
➤ If you don't take action, you go back to Step 4.
➤ Then you come back to Step 5.

For example,

➤ You realize you want to buy a rental property in your town.
➤ You have set up a list of people who are renting out their properties.
➤ You set up your schedule to call these phone numbers.
   o Alternative A – You call ten people, reach five

137

people, and they all turn you down. Learn how to sell better by listening to sales training courses. Many of these are in your local library or can be purchased online.

o   Alternative B – You call three people, get their answering machines, and quit. Now you go back to Step 4 and return to Step 5.

Here is more great news. Your first phone call is your worst phone call. It only gets better from here.

Your breakthrough comes when you either get the result or the insight about what is missing for you to get the result.

Step 6

Step 6 is to acknowledge yourself. Acknowledge yourself for taking action. I suggest that each day, you journal:

- ➤ What worked
- ➤ What didn't work
- ➤ What you learned
- ➤ What you are going to do tomorrow

This could be long pages of notes or it could be a couple of bullet points. Sometimes I jot down my rehab milestones in my calendar, for example. You could use a gratitude journal to write down what you are thankful for each day. Did you consider that you can be grateful for lessons learned from negative events or experiences?

If you don't like to write, you can verbally acknowledge yourself for what you have accomplished and what you have learned. You can say it to yourself or your spouse or friend or accountability partner or mentor.

This step is important. Over the years, I have found that this acknowledgement has accelerated my growth and development versus other associates of mine. Please realize that sometimes your accomplishments are small; however, they build on each other.

My contractor tells me:

> Rehabbers love the beginning of the project because
> you see big changes like walls being knocked down
> and cabinets being removed. When we get into the
> nitty gritty of the project and it takes us three hours to
> solve a foundation problem or an hour to make sure
> the countertop lines up perfectly, you are not happy.
> However, it is the little things that add up to a quality
> and profit-making project.

While listening to *Unleash the Power Within*,[29] I heard Tony
Robbins say something like this:

> If you improve 1% a day, then in one year you will have
> improved 365%. That is a full circle!

Brag on yourself. Brag on social media, with your friends, with
your coach. Let people know the growth that you have each and
every day and the progress you're making each and every day.

Success breeds success. You not only gain confidence by doing
this step. You will also generate referrals for sellers, buyers and
private lenders.

Do something fun! It does not have to be expensive. All your
mind wants to do is to celebrate and any kind of celebration will
work. When you celebrate, you create more dopamine in your
brain. For example, you could get a massage or take the family
for an outing or take the weekend off.

> Dopamine motivates you to take action toward your goals,
> desires, and needs, and gives you a surge of reinforcing
> pleasure when achieving them. Procrastination, self-
> doubt, and lack of enthusiasm are linked with low levels
> of dopamine.

Break big goals down into little pieces—rather than

---

29 Robbins, Anthony, *Unleash the Power Within*, Nightingale Conant, 1999.

only allowing your brain to celebrate when you've hit the finish line, you can create a series of little finish-lines which releases dopamine. And it's crucial to actually celebrate—buy a bottle of wine, or head to your favorite restaurant whenever you meet a small goal.

And avoid the dopamine hangover; when you tank out after a massive high. Create new goals before achieving your current one. That ensures a consistent pattern for experiencing dopamine. As an employer and leader, recognize the accomplishments of your team. Sending an encouraging email, or giving a bonus, will allow them to have a dopamine hit and increase future motivation and productivity. [30]

Step 7

Step 7: do it again!

Take your profits and reinvest it in your business, so that you can accelerate your growth.

Take on the next challenge or breakthrough and repeat success.

Buy another rehab or rental. Wholesale another property. Add buyers, sellers and private lenders to your list.

That's right. Just like shampoo:

Lather, rinse and repeat success.

Here is a chart to use while going through this process:

---

30 "Hacking Into Your Happy Chemicals: Dopamine, Serotonin, Endorphins, & Oxytocin" theutopianlife.com/2014/10/14/hacking-into-your-happy-chemicals-dopamine-serotonin-endorphins-oxytocin (accessed July 16 2016).

Step 1: Area of focus	
Step 2: Where am I right now regarding _____?	
Step 3: What's my goal?	
Step 4: What's my block? What's limiting me?	The problem is_____ I can't because_____ It's hard because_____ I tried but_____ I don't know how to_____ I don't have time to_____
Step 5: Three action steps I will take to accomplish my goal	1. _____ 2. _____ 3. _____
Step 6: Acknowledge what I learned and acknowledge my success	
Step 7: Do it again: Here is my next goal or area of focus	

So (almost) all you really need to know about real estate, you've learned through life

REMEMBER THE BOOK *All I Really Need to Know, I Learned in Kindergarten* by Robert Fulghum?[31]

My goal with this book is to help you to see you already have many skills that will allow you to be successful in real estate. That is why I say that (almost) all you really need to know about real estate, you have learned through life.

And there are many aptitudes specific to women that can really help us be successful.

---

31 Fulghum, Robert, *All I Really Need to Know, I Learned in Kindergarten,* Ballantine, 2004.

Of course, there is specialized knowledge you need to learn. And some of that we have disclosed here. As we go through our series of books, you will peel through the layers of the onion to gather much of this specialized knowledge.

The rest of it, as Henry Ford said, you can hire people to provide for you.

So congratulations!

You are well on your way to having financial freedom through real estate!

What's next?

Please join me for the next book: *Women Are Simply Better at Getting Started in Real Estate.*

This book gives you a detailed overview of how to invest in real estate. I will show you:

➤ Twelve ways to find off-market deals

➤ How to analyze the numbers for a house you want to buy, fix and sell

➤ How to analyze the numbers for a rental property

➤ How to walk through a property and create your scope of work

➤ How to print money in your basement (well, not exactly) by putting a property under contract and assigning it to someone else

➤ How to market your property for sale

➤ How to market your property if you are renting it

➤ How to have multiple exit strategies so you reduce your risk when owning real estate

And much, much more

I invite you to visit **www.WomenAreSimplyBetterAtIt.com** to receive real estate and business resources, read excerpts and blog posts, and see news about upcoming books. Feel free to share your feedback and progress. I look forward to seeing you there and sharing your journey to success!

About the author

Linda Baumgarten has been an entrepreneur for over twenty years: technical writer, insurance agent, real estate investor, business consultant, motivational speaker, course designer, and real estate/business coach.

She has achieved the pinnacle of success in each of the companies for which she has worked or created. As an insurance agent, she was a $3 million dollar producer selling insurance one family at a time. For over seven years, Business Network International acknowledged Baumgarten as the top networker in her chapter. Linda effectively worked with over 100 volunteers to become the number one communication course manager in the country at Landmark Education Corporation.

Linda steps in when she sees a need. Feeling that small businesses were underserved in her local Chamber of Commerce, she created the Small Business Council and Webster Small Business of the Year Annual Award. As a volunteer, she uses her marketing skills to help animal rescues raise needed funds and find homes for homeless cats and dogs.

Baumgarten has been interviewed on television, radio, in the newspaper about investing in real estate. She has insp thousands of people to realize their dreams of financial freedor the Connecticut Real Estate Investors Association and around country. As one of its coaches, she is proud that CT REIA has b acknowledged as one of the Best Real Estate Educational Provic by the Commercial Record.

Baumgarten was awarded the Women of FIRE (Finar Insurance, and Real Estate) Award by Banker & Tradesman being among the most talented, ambitious, and innovative wor entrepreneurs in Connecticut.

In *Why Women Are Simply Better at Real Estate,* you discover that Linda's living principle is that ordinary people extraordinary. She strives to recognize and empower succ making qualities in each person she meets and coaches. students and business clients overwhelmingly achieve t business and life goals.

Now it is your turn to benefit from her teachings and practica words of empowerment in the exciting world of real estate.

Made in the USA
Middletown, DE
29 July 2017